VOLUME 3 IN THE DEATH WALKER SERIES

WALKABOUT
THE FURTHER MULTIDIMENSIONAL ADVENTURES WITH WYRME AND ANDY

GALEN STOLLER
EDITOR: K PAUL STOLLER, MD / FOREWORD: RICHARD MARTINI

Walkabout: The Further Multidimensional Adventures with Andy & Wyrme
Copyright © 2025 by K. Paul Stoller

For more about this author please visit https://www.dreamtreaderpress.com/

Cover Design Image(s) provided by the author

This author is not engaged in rendering medical or psychological services, and this book is not intended as a guide to diagnose or treat medical or psychological problems. If you require medical, psychological, or other expert assistance, please seek the services of your own physician or mental health professional.

All rights reserved. No part of this publication may be reproduced, distributed, or transmitted in any form or by any means, including photocopying, recording, or other electronic or mechanical methods, without the prior written permission of the author, except in the case of brief quotations embodied in critical reviews and certain other noncommercial uses permitted by copyright law. Please do not participate in or encourage piracy of copyrighted materials in violation of the author's rights.

No part of this book may be used for the training of artificial systems, including systems based on artificial intelligence (AI), without the copyright owner's prior permission. This prohibition shall be in force even on platforms and systems that claim to have such rights based on an implied contract for hosting the book.

Paperback ISBN: 978-0-9832425-8-1
Hardcover ISBN: 978-0-9882027-6-4

1. Main category—Religion & Spirituality › Spirituality › Personal Growth › Transformational
2. Other category—Religion & Spirituality › New Age › Channeling
3. Other category—Religion & Spirituality › New Age › Self-Help

Published by: Dream Treader Press
K. Paul Stoller, Publisher
DreamTreaderPress.com
With American Real Publishing
americanrealpublishing.com

TABLE OF CONTENTS

Foreword v

Prologue 1

Chapter 1: School 7

Chapter 2: Portals 101 17

Chapter 3: Through Andy's Eyes 25

Chapter 4: The Orb 33

Chapter 5: Wyrme's Arrival 41

Chapter 6: The Dark Blob 53

Chapter 7: Bridges Between Beings 63

Chapter 8: The Shimmering 73

Chapter 9: Pursuit of the Self 83

Chapter 10: Agreement with Glen 93

Chapter 11: The Land of Denial 105

Chapter 12: Realm of the Water People 117

Chapter 13: Realm of Love 125

Chapter 14: The City of "Like Hindsight" 135

Chapter 15: The Golden Revolving Door 143

Chapter 16: The Stone Clackers 153

Epilogue 163

About the Author 169

About the Editor 170

FOREWORD

A DECADE AGO, I WAS INVITED to participate in the Hollywood Book Festival, where filmmakers connect with authors to see if their books might make interesting films or TV projects. Because of my background in film, festival founder Bruce Haring asked me to look at some books that had been selected as finalists. I was fortunate to read *My Life After Life: A Posthumous Memoir*, the first of a series written by Galen Stoller, who had died in a train accident, and edited by his father, Dr. Ken Stoller. As I read the narrative, a chill went up my spine, as I recognized information in Galen's story that echoed aspects of the research for my documentary, *Flipside: A Journey into the Afterlife*, based on what thousands of people have said under deep hypnosis about the afterlife.

Curious if Galen's father Ken was familiar with this research, I reached out to him. He confirmed that neither he nor his son had heard of it, so Galen's accounts of classrooms in the afterlife, a notion that had profoundly affected me during my own research, didn't come from any source other than Galen himself.

The idea of classrooms in the afterlife would give anyone pause, especially those who relished graduating from college assuming they'd never have to take another class again. Of course, these classrooms aren't made of brick and mortar, and each person who experiences them has their own point of reference for explaining their function and appearance. But I first started hearing about classrooms in the afterlife from a friend who had a recurring dream similar to James Van Praagh's accounts in his book *Talking to Heaven*.

One day my friend said, "I think I'm going to another galaxy." When I asked her why she thought that, she replied, "I have this recurring dream that I'm in a classroom in another galaxy. Everyone is dressed in white; they're speaking a language I've never heard before but that I completely understand." The night after she passed, I got a call from an old friend of hers who said, "I had this wonderful dream, in which our friend was in the "fourth dimension" in a classroom where everyone was dressed in white. She seemed very happy."

A few years later I ran across Michael Newton's *Journey of Souls*, in which a person under deep hypnosis recounted being in a classroom in the afterlife, which eventually led me to begin work on my documentary and book on the topic.

Subsequently, I filmed a number of between-life sessions, two of which included visits to my departed friend in her classroom in the afterlife, as well as to other classrooms.

But it wasn't until I read *My Life After Life* that I heard a first-person account of a student who was in one of these classrooms, describing his feelings about going to class, the other students in the classroom, and the life lessons they were learning *in the afterlife*.

I saw *My Life After Life* as a wonderful film about the Stoller family's journey, and how the death of their son was not the end of their story but, in fact, only the beginning. Consequently, I arranged to option the film rights to see if I could convince any of my film business contacts to consider this project as a film or TV series.

Trying to pitch Galen's story, however, one jaded exec said, "Oh, come on. This young boy was in a train accident, and the book comes out of his bereft father's desire to change that reality." That's exactly what I would expect a film exec to say, but there is greater truth in Galen and Ken's books. For any parent who has lost a child, Galen's story gives radiant hope and, if embraced, will change their lives forever.

I've now read all three books in the series, and each one interweaves with and touches upon revelations in the others. I've also come to know Ken, the doctor and the father, who helps fan the flame of his son's creativity. What's arresting about Ken's approach as editor is his ability to let his son tell his story—"Here's what I saw, here's what I experienced"—even though it doesn't fit neatly into a traditional narrative, despite its breathtaking scope.

The first book focuses on Galen's journey to the other world; the second book deals with people he meets there;

and this third one explores various realms he can access. To be with Galen when he approaches other people in the afterlife, with all the aplomb a sixteen-year-old in the afterlife can muster, is fascinating. Especially memorable is the account of a family who died in the Indonesian tsunami, people still carrying memories of their religion and background without being sure where they are.

In Galen's latest book, *Walkabout*, a title that brings to mind the rite of passage native male indigenous Australians (Aborigines) undergo during adolescence when they live in the wilderness, we find a young man with a keen eye giving us a guided tour of where he is in the afterlife and what other realms he is able to access. I've heard reference to these other realms in the research of Michael Newton or near-death experience research, but never in such vivid detail.

It's a bit like reading the *Odyssey* for the first time, with its tales of sirens and monsters and other creatures in the great unknown world of ancient Greece. While there isn't the obvious story line where good conquers evil, there is a story line where knowledge helps determine the next step in Galen's rite of passage—as if the realms he visits are like the classes he took in *My Life After Life*, each one with distinct lessons in integrity, curiosity, and willingness to examine what exists, rather than what we might expect.

Similarly, Ken forwarded an email that he received from a woman in St. Louis, Missouri, who wrote that her husband had recently passed away, and because it was difficult for her to continue living, she visited a psychic to see if she could speak to her departed loved one. She reported: "I first heard about Galen's book from my husband, who is on the other side. I was having a reading, and Bob started describing a book with a red and green cover and gave the title. The [medium] hadn't heard about it because it had just been published. I got the book, read it as fast as I could…then at the next reading I had with my husband, we discussed it. He wanted me to have more insight into what it was like where he is now, although he stressed that it wasn't just like Galen's environment, but close. Thank you so very much for getting this book published and out to all of us who need to read it." Since neither she nor the medium had prior knowledge of Galen's book, how could the medium reveal such information? To my mind, the answer is obvious: We are more connected to the spirit realm than we think.

Reportedly, Steve Jobs's last words were, "Oh wow. Oh wow. Oh wow." Could it be that he was getting a glimpse of this other world? I happen to think so.

I believe every one of us has our own journey, and wherever we wind up it's for our benefit, for our learning, which fits whatever part of the journey we are on. Galen's stories about the realms he visits, which echo Tibetan monks' accounts of the realms they go to through deep meditation, or the revelations about near-death experiences by people who claim to have witnessed similar realms, are the first detailed, first-person accounts in print of what it's like to be in such realms, and, as such, they are thrilling to read. For that I thank Ken for being open and receptive enough to help his son tell this story, despite his own trying journey following his son's death.

And I thank Galen, who as a talented performer as witnessed by his YouTube videos, has found a way to speak to his father from the great beyond and teach us a lesson or two.

—Richard Martini

Richard Martini is an award-winning filmmaker and journalist who has written and/or directed a number of feature films and documentaries, including the book and documentary *Flipside: A Tourist's Guide on How to Navigate the Afterlife*.

PROLOGUE

While I am having a lot of fun where I am, just as I had a lot of fun on earth, an ongoing concern is to avoid making life in this dimension sound appealing as an alternative to a boring life on earth. Had I been able to live on, I would have chosen to stay on earth to continue having experiences and learning there before coming here. This dimension is not just a wonderland or playground. I have had doubts and fears at times, like any human on earth would, because human qualities exist in this space as well, and it is necessary to learn and develop on the other side also. I also want to stress that the experiences I'm having here are not available to everyone who crosses over, especially those who might commit suicide thinking the other side might allow them such experiences. Suicide does *not* get people to a place of beauty and interesting activities. On the contrary, people who commit suicide become trapped and have to work through past experiences in a completely different way for an uncomfortable duration. In fact, the act of suicide is treated here like a disease in the sense that such people are literally quarantined, as if they were contagious. And even when they are released from such confinement, their freedom is limited in certain ways in comparison to that of individuals who arrive here naturally.

Further, even when people arrive here naturally, they have different experiences, depending on their circumstances and experiences in their prior lives. So my books simply contain accounts of my own experiences. Not everyone is provided with a Wyrme or an Andy to aid their orientation and the adaptation when they come into this dimension. For example, the young woman I called Monica, who stood in front of a tree and just stared[1], illustrates how individuals have completely different experiences in this dimension according to what events and tendencies were set into motion during their earth lives. People cannot predetermine what experiences they will have here, especially if they alter the natural path of their lives.

However, my intention in writing my books is to help people prepare themselves as much as possible for this dimension by viewing my experiences as templates for ones they could potentially encounter.

Editor's note: As Galen notes, the types of experiences people have on the other side are determined by the kinds of experiences and tendencies they had on earth. So because Galen was always very imaginative and creative on earth, he continues to have these qualities in his new

---

[1] Described in the entitled "Monica" in *Life Chapters*.

dimension. While living on earth, he saw beyond the limitations in front of him to other possibilities, and he carried this tendency into his new dimension. Another person, such as one who had more fearful experiences while on earth, would have different experiences on the other side, as well as different lessons to learn. However, Galen's observations and experiences can provide insights into the nature of the other side and the types of conditions and activities others who cross over might face.

Reality follows certain laws regardless of what realm we are in. While each level and layer of reality may have its own laws, there are universal laws that are consistent throughout in all realms. Disrespect for life violates the universal laws and has consequences, no matter what level people are on. There are no hiding places in our universe, and nobody gets away with violating a universal law.

We are not born on this planet to prepare for death, but are here to have experiences in the classroom that is earth. Such experiences can increase our awareness of what awaits us when we do leave, as well as make us more conscious of the opportunities available *here* before we depart. As we become more conscious, we take more seriously our individual and collective responsibilities to other beings in various dimensions, and so we have the opportunity to become better stewards of the biosphere that supports human life, realizing that the earth will do fine without us, as I have been assured. But we will not be able to exist as earth humans, continuing to learn in the classroom of earth, if we foolishly destroy our environment.

CHAPTER 1

SCHOOL

School was where I first realized that I was not limited in my new dimension, even in what has become my everyday life here. School is also where I initially discovered there were many types of beings with whom I could interact, regardless of their origins or appearance, and this has been one of my greatest joys in this dimension. My first day at school reflects how my perspective could often be expanded.

That morning, the morning of that first day of school, I felt pulled to be somewhere after getting out of bed. By that time I had created a home—a small log cabin much like the guest cabins at a national park in the western United States, reflecting my desire to hold onto the possibility, even if remote, that I was just on a sort of "vacation," and that at some point I would go back home. Even my bed was made of logs, with a mattress on top covered by a homey quilt of red and green flannel. There was also a small table with two chairs and a potbellied stove, in which I would occasionally build a fire for cheer, even though I was never actually cold.

After getting dressed, I walked out the front door of my cabin, knowing that if something wanted me to be somewhere, I would be guided to where I needed to be. Then suddenly, as if being pulled by a powerful magnet, I was turned around and my feet just started to walk in a certain direction, with a strong feeling of having received a message. I remembered having had this feeling before, but on earth the experience of being pulled had been mental, like being drawn by my imagination, while here the experience of being pulled in a certain direction felt much more physical, to the point where my feet seemed to have a mind of their own.

As I walked on, crossing the paths of many people, I sensed there were others also being drawn to the same location, all moving with the same rhythm as me. Soon I was closing in on a large building with beautiful, delicate architecture that would not have held up under conditions on earth, generally modern in appearance but also having many elements of old architecture—such as flying buttresses. Seeing the building and not yet knowing it was a school, I thought perhaps there was something else being issued to new arrivals in addition to our cups.

As I arrived at the building, I made myself a little more presentable by running my hand through my hair to make sure it was in place.

Then I walked through the doors, and a magnificent feeling of both belonging and expansion came over me. For one fleeting second, the most pleasant feeling I had ever experienced ran through my body. It felt like space opened up, and I sensed that I had the potential to know everything.

I walked down a long hall that looked like it went on forever, while ahead of me others filed into various rooms. Then, as I passed one door, I was pulled into a room, as if a vacuum were sucking me in. Looking around, I was surprised to see a classroom with desks, a chalkboard, books, and notepads. Everything looked familiar to me, just what one would expect in a classroom on earth.

I realized that I must be going to school, and with quiet anticipation I sat down at a desk while looking at the ten other people around me, some slumped down in their chairs, others sitting up alert, and others reading. I felt awkward and unprepared, because, unlike the others, I hadn't brought anything with me with which to take notes. When I asked the person closest to me if I could borrow some paper and a pen, he looked at me with a confused expression, as if he was saying, "Why are you asking me this?"

"I didn't know I was coming to school, so I am unprepared," I said in response.

The guy shook his head with a laugh and replied, "You will be fine. Don't worry about it."

When I focused attention again on my desk, there on it was exactly what I needed—two books, a pad of paper, and pens. I realized that apparently, when you go to school here, you are automatically provided with everything you need.

When the teacher came in, I was almost overwhelmed by his apparent strength and energy. I felt like I was sitting in front of one of the most magnificent, awe-inspiring persons you could ever hope to meet. Only later did I learn that such teachers are angels, a band of beings in service to those who utilize incarnate experience to evolve.

Although this teacher's appearance was plain—he was about five feet, two inches tall with a slight build and almost no hair on his head—his powerful presence seemed to fill the entire room. Nothing about the way he looked could have led me to believe that he possessed the energy that I felt. Only the fact that such teachers are angels accounted for why energy seemed so different and powerful. It was one of the first times I had a "things are not what they seem moment." Subsequently, I increasingly realized that there can be a very big difference between how things appear and how things feel in this dimension.

The teacher began the class with introductory statements, as if this was the first class of the first year for new arrivals, so apparently we were all on the same level of learning. Then he spoke about how people can use their intuition and intentions to move energy in this and other dimensions, emphasizing how this was one of the greatest tools we had here. He then spoke about how, in other dimensions, universal laws had been created by various councils, one such law being that illusion is not a true foundation for energy.

As I listened to him, I pictured what he was describing, imagining a planet with great beings conversing about how illusion can serve individuals or how polarity operates on earth. The discussion these great councils may have had revolved around the fact that some individuals could choose a life of illusion, never facing reality, yet still do fine, while others could seek out reality, trying to understand the nature of energy and their relationship to their souls and the greater universe. Also the teacher said that because of free will someone living on earth could *choose* to follow universal truth. I could see how these two schools of thought, this polarity, played out on earth, including in my own life with family and friends. It amazed me that I could have such a rich experience in this classroom as a result of just hearing a few words from this teacher.

When it came time to end his lecture, the teacher asked, "Does anyone have any questions, or is there anything else you would like to talk about?"

I raised my hand and said, "I came from a place where such polarity exists in daily life."

"Yes, you are from earth, and there are a few others here from earth as well," the teacher replied. Looking around the room, I saw a few heads nodding, although I didn't realize the implications of what the teacher had just said until later.

"Does polarity exist on many other planets?" I asked.

"There are many planets where there are varying degrees of polarity, but the earth is the place of greatest experimentation with polarity, because it has the most pull between free will and universal truth. There are other planets that are very much like the dimension we're in now, with no polarity, but on them individuals still have free will and choice. Earth is a very interesting experiment, don't you agree?"

I started to laugh, as I was really able to see that there *was* a great experiment of polarity occurring on earth. Of course, when on earth, there is a sense that the way earth operates is all there is, but in truth elsewhere, as in my dimension, there is no polarity and seemingly endless potential choices are available. It is even possible to move out of polarity while living in a dimension of polarity such as on earth.

I thanked the teacher, and as I watched him leave, I felt the powerful energy in the room diminish. Everyone left their seats and milled around, and I introduced myself to a few people who looked interesting. When I went to grab my books and the notes I had taken, they were gone. I left the wonderful building thinking about what I had learned and how amazing it was to be in a class where I could visualize the lesson, as if it were a movie being screened in front of me. Halfway back home I stopped abruptly when I suddenly realized the implications of what the teacher had said with the phrase "a few of you are from earth." This clearly meant that some others were not from earth, and I had probably interacted with beings from other planets or realms. This was exciting to me and made me curious about where the others might be from. Everyone there had looked like a human being, including the teacher, though clearly he was not, as I had never met a human with that kind of energy.

At that moment I realized for the first time that the dimension I am in wasn't just a place that earthlings occupied. My imagination ran wild as I now scrutinized everyone more closely, but no one looked any different from people I would see on earth, and nothing gave me a clue that others were not from the earth. Still, the idea that I might have met someone from another planet thrilled me. Before going home I sat at my favorite rock on my hill and thought more about whether any of the students who had attended the class had seemed different and the implications of some not being from earth. It then occurred to me that people are earthlings if they live on earth, but that doesn't mean that is where they came from. I had never before considered the possibility that there might be lots of aliens living on earth. But now I *know* it is probably true, because in the dimension where I now live, it *is* true. All these ideas made me sense the potential for learning here.

Editor's note: To Galen, the short, slight, balding teacher who, despite his size, projected great power and energy was the very image of polarity, so he was a catalyst for reflecting on the polarity that characterizes earth life, as well as the deceptiveness of appearances.

At this early point in Galen's sojourn, he was still coming to understand himself and his dimension, so things sometimes seemed very surreal to him. He told me his experience was like in *The Wizard of Oz*, where Dorothy's intention is to go home someday, so he felt his log cabin, though warm and cozy, was small and temporary. On one level, we are all on holiday, since life on earth is not permanent. One of the illusions some humans have on earth is that because they are present on earth *now*, some aspect of them should *always* be present on earth, so they erect buildings adorned with their names and have busts or statues made of their likenesses. But there is no permanence of any kind on earth, and any of us could be gone in the next instant. Any pharaoh who has crossed over would likely tell us that no number of statues, obelisks, or well-adorned tombs will keep anything about us present on earth or provide us with any assurance about where we will end up after death, even though that was the belief of the pharaohs on earth.

Yet even though our life on earth is impermanent, our desire to learn, contribute, and be responsible members of our families, the larger family of man, and beyond is an eternal quest. There is more to life than just getting up, going to work, coming home, and going to bed. Life is not static; it is constantly changing, and it offers potentially infinite possibilities. If we take a moment every day to ask ourselves, "What is special about today, and what can I learn from being present in it?" we might learn a great deal about ourselves and our destiny before we depart earth.

CHAPTER 2

PORTALS 101

I'd thought that in this dimension you just had to figure everything out as you went, so it gave me such a sense of joy to know that there was an educational system that could explain the experiences I had been having. I always liked to learn, and for a moment I wondered if this was something I had created. But everyone here feels a connection to this school, so it does not exist only because I died when I was a teenager who had been going to school and therefore expected to find one here.

As time passed, I would sense, first thing in the morning, whether I would be attending school that day. And if it was a school day, I would anticipate school enthusiastically, because it meant being exposed to different ideas, teachers, and classmates. I also came to understand that the lessons taught to me were linked to aspects of this dimension I'd been curious about, so there was continuity in my learning.

Many of the lesson topics at school were familiar—either I'd read about such subjects while on earth, or heard about them from my father, or knew about them instinctively—but they were further explained in classes. In fact, of the students attending classes with me, no one was ever surprised by the topics discussed, because it seemed we all had the same level of understanding.

An important aspect of my education in this dimension has been learning to distinguish between what existed naturally here and what was a projection of my own needs and desires. In the beginning I had to develop the ability to discern such differences. For example, it gave me a sense of comfort to have Andy with me, because I love dogs. So for a long time I thought I might have created Andy. When I took the time to really see that Andy was separate from me—a being with his own understandings and experiences—it was a profound discovery. As a result, I could see how people on earth often made the mistake of feeling they owned things or people around them due to their inability to distinguish between their needs and the separate energy and wisdom belonging to independent persons, animals, or property.

After a while, I began to recognize the difference between projections of my needs and separate entities having their own spirits. In this way I eventually learned that school here was not a projection of my needs, but that it exists to serve the growth of the entire community.

So every morning when I woke and felt drawn to school, I was delighted. I would run gleefully toward the building with Andy barking behind me. I noticed that Andy would never come into the building, and at the beginning I just thought dogs didn't go to school, and I didn't question it. Later, when I found out that Andy was very conscious, I realized that Andy was part of the school and didn't need to be *in* it. In fact, some of the teachers had energy that felt very much like Andy's.

Once at school, I would be drawn to a particular classroom and finally to a specific seat in the room, a process that seemed like a game. Many of the lessons taught there were fascinating, not only providing useful information but also actual experiences that illustrated some of the principles being taught. For example, a class on the nature of portals to other dimensions began with a visual demonstration of the changes in energy levels and patterns that can accompany experiences of going through portals. Before the lecture, everything in the classroom took on a surreal energy, so the classroom looked like the static on an old TV with an analog broadcast. Everything appeared distorted, and although the scene was still in color, forms had the unclear resolution of an old videotape.

Surveying the classroom, I could see most of the other students were having the same experience of perceiving everything as fuzzy static. However, two girls sitting together in the front row, identical twins dressed exactly the same, were acting like the phenomenon was no big deal, making me wonder if *they* were projections in this TV land.

Soon the teacher's theatrical entrance added to the special effects. He came in with lightning dancing through misty clouds rolling up from the floor to his feet, the atmosphere making his entrance seem more like a magic act than real.

The teacher also looked exactly like a wizard who could direct and change energy levels, with white hair and sculpted beard—although he was not dressed like a wizard. Instead, he wore a corduroy jacket with leather patches on the elbows, like a typical college professor on earth. After making a theatrical pause while he scanned the audience, he said in a clear dramatic voice, "Today, class, we are going to learn about portals."

I was thrilled that I would learn something other than a practical lesson about how to treat someone or another universal law.

The teacher then described what portals were and their purpose in the universe. He said portals were passages through space-time into another dimension or realm of consciousness, and although portals can physically take you to other dimensions, it was not always necessary to leave physical space to enter into a portal and travel, as daydreams can also be portals to other realms. The teacher also emphasized that portals must be respected and not misused, saying, "I caution you not to try to step through portals until you have a little more experience controlling your own energy and a better understanding of the field of energy that you currently occupy."

He added that many of us were still very new here, although some had already traveled through portals. And then he looked at the twins and said, "Daydream away like you have done before you came to this dimension, but understand that when you step through portals, you can literally rearrange your energy field and create confusion, so caution is required." I was curious about what might happen in such an event, imagining goo on the floor like a horrific transporter accident in *Star Trek*.

Then the teacher continued, saying, "Portals have always been here and are part of the fabric of the universe. Just like there are reasons for the pores on your skin, portals, which are pathways that make up the space around us, have functions. And there are beings who tend portals—hold these spaces for travelers to move through them—and thus help maintain the functions of these portals."

At the end of his lecture, the teacher left in the same dramatic way in which he had arrived, and I felt like applauding his theatrical performance. The class enhanced my curiosity about portals more than giving me final answers about them, as if the teacher had challenged the students to further investigate the nature of portals. I felt the need to push the envelope and explore portals. Of course, I had heard the teacher's warning to be cautious, but it wasn't until later that I understood exactly why. Still, if I had not followed my urge to explore portals, I likely would never have encountered Wyrme, a creature that has not only been a wonderful companion but has also further sparked my curiosity about the universe, imagination, and journeys to other realms.

CHAPTER 3

THROUGH ANDY'S EYES

As I left the school, I couldn't wait to discover my first portal. I went to my favorite space, the green hillside with the rock I liked to lean up against, to scan the horizon, thinking that if I could see a portal, I could understand them better, discover how to enter one. But I did not see anything resembling a portal around the horizon. After that I walked around looking at objects closely to see if I could spot movement indicating that they were portals. I assumed the energy around portals must be swirling, like spirals, or at least disturbed in some way. When I did this, Andy would look where I did and cock his head at me as if to say, "What are you looking for?" So it became a game for us. But I didn't see anything doing this either.

Next, instead of looking for something I could walk up to or something on the horizon, I tried to soften my vision, and then I discovered something wonderful. I could see a golden light shimmering around everything in my field of vision. Again, Andy tried to figure out what I was looking at, although I assumed he realized what I was trying to do because he put his big paw on my chest, jarring me a little. Not wanting to play with him at the time, I made him lie down and returned to watching the shimmering energy around everything. Soon Andy began to get more insistent in his attempts to distract me.

Frustrated, I decided that maybe if I closed my eyes and meditated to myself, I might be able to locate a portal. So I leaned up against my rock, relaxed into a meditation position, and started to follow my breath. Andy stopped trying to get my attention. I could feel my body, with my back against the rock and legs in the grass, as well as my breath and Andy's breath. From there I started to expand my awareness.

Then, suddenly, it felt like I flipped in the air. I opened my eyes and found myself lying on the ground looking up at the sky, with no idea how I got there or what brought me out of that quiet space. When I sat up, I was facing the rock on which I had been leaning. Clearly something had flipped me around. I looked at Andy, who was sitting next to the rock, and I swear he smiled as if to say, "Are you happy now?"

I sat back down to meditate more, but I couldn't achieve the same state of relaxation, because I was too self-conscious—my mind was expecting something to happen, and I wanted to witness it at the moment it occurred. I realized that knowing that something happened and waiting for it to happen again actually diminishes the possibility that it will happen, while being open and peaceful aligns you to the energy field around you, increasing the possibility that a phenomenon will recur. So I developed the patience to move into a quiet space *without expectation*. For days on end I practiced this, and at times I was in a state of near *samadhi*[2], but I never again had the experience of my body being flipped around, and I remained uncertain about what had actually happened.

After a few days, I resumed my normal activities, returning to school, but my focus was still on my driving need to discover portals. I had no idea why I was so obsessed with this. Perhaps because it was about travel, having different experiences, or testing science and belief, things I had always loved. One thing was certain—the calmer I became, the more I connected to other energy, while the more obsessed I became about looking for portals, the less I was able to relate to the energy around me. Clearly, I needed to find the balance between looking for portals and being relaxed enough to find them. And that was how I eventually discovered my first portal.

One day when I was petting Andy, who often tugged on my jacket, trying to engage me during my attempts to discover portals, I grabbed his face, looked into his eyes, and said, "Where exactly do you go when you are not with me?" Andy grounded me in my new home, and without Andy around I didn't feel the same energy field, so it was natural for me to wonder if he went to another dimension when he disappeared on jaunts. As I looked into his eyes, I could feel myself being drawn into that space and could see what was inside them—an incred-

2 *Samadhi* is a Sanskrit word for a high level of concentrated meditation, as well as a heightened awareness of our connectedness.

ible intelligence communicating to me on a different level. I realized that Andy was now communicating with me through energetic exchange in a way that allowed me to see his energy level.

I was now entering into a beautiful field of energy that I perceived visually as a pleasant soft brown color surrounding me, which likely was influenced by the color of Andy's eyes. It felt like I was floating backward weightless, with no sense of gravity, which was a joyful experience. Although in my dimension I could have created a weightless environment if I'd wanted that, I was participating in this experience, not creating it. In one corner of the soft brown area, there was a space that seemed to lead somewhere, and I tried to get to that space. But I was suddenly jerked back to my previous reality as Andy lunged forward to lick my face and barked at me as if to wake me up. Nevertheless, I was certain that I had just had my first experience going through a portal, even though it had occurred in a split second.

I was thrilled and grabbed Andy's face again and looked into his eyes, this time not so much to enter that space again but to express to him that I now knew he was not just a dog, now really understanding that things aren't what they appear to be here. I tried unsuccessfully to get Andy to engage with me again on this different level, such as saying something to me, but still after that day, he looked into my eyes more frequently and never again was I able to think of Andy as just a dog, but instead as more of a teacher.

This first experience with portals, catalyzed by looking into Andy's eyes, felt safe because I was familiar with the color of his eyes. I realized that Andy had likely protected me from moving toward that dark corner area, because whatever was there would not have served me at that time. In this way, Andy prevented me from having an experience for which I was not prepared, but without giving me a clear understanding of limitations.

The feeling I had while exploring the portal of Andy's eyes was of having connected again with a part of myself that I had long forgotten. This feeling made me want to further explore portals—to not only discover new realms, but also more about my inner realms.

Editor's note: Portals are not just holes in the universe like one would find in Swiss cheese. They do not open and close according to our will; they appear when people have a need for them that serves a purpose beyond mere curiosity. Portals are everywhere, but they are primarily inside ourselves. A companion can help us open the portals, because love for others is a key that opens them. Andy's love for Galen, and his choice to be companion and teacher, gave Andy the opportunity to teach Galen how to work with portals and discover their function. And it was the affection they both shared for each other that opened the first portal observed by Galen. Andy assisted Galen in the experience and kept Galen safe due to love, as if he had been a toddler out on his own lawn during his earth life being watched carefully by me—his father. This experience helped Galen prepare for that day when he would encounter another, universal-class traveling companion—Wyrme.

CHAPTER 4

THE ORB

As time went on, it became clearer to me that it is our understanding of who we are and why we are here that helps us move through portals. So the next time I was ready to try to go through a portal, I said to Andy, "I really want to explore a portal again and understand the process, because it feels like such a part of understanding myself."

Andy looked at me and cocked his head, as if to affirm what I had said. That's when I realized that I had made an agreement, on Andy's terms, about traversing portals. I followed the same steps as before. I held Andy's face, looked in his eyes, and waited to be absorbed into that space. Andy returned my gaze with patience and openness, but all I was able to experience was wet hands from holding Andy's jaw. I was beside myself, and, of course, Andy couldn't tell me what was going on, because he didn't speak. Frustrated and insistent on traversing a portal again, I sat with Andy for a long time and began to feel the energy drawing me forward, but then it stopped. I repeated these attempts several times, which only bored Andy, who tried to meander off while I kept pulling him back.

Then I remembered the feeling I had had when I was first drawn in to the portal—not the excitement of wondering where I was going or expectation of certain things about to happen, but the excitement of *being*. When I remembered this, everything started to vibrate faster, and I realized that if I could maintain the excitement without expectation of where I was going, I could traverse a portal.

It was the hardest practice I had ever done, because I had to remain open and maintain an expectation of energy without expecting specific results. I understood why individuals who travel through portals are considered masters, because it is not easy. Eventually I realized that the more I let go of expectations, the more I was again drawn through the portal of Andy's eyes.

After I arrived in that space for the second time, Andy contained me in an orb of energy with him. It was like looking through a crystal ball from inside it. Later I found out that it is not necessary to have a container to move through portals, but that Andy had created one for my safety, so I couldn't get lost, since I was a beginner at traversing portals. In this orb of energy, I could see Andy, who showed me how to move by example. He would repeatedly look at me, then look ahead, giving me a silent message in a way very unlike a dog. I laughed because seeing him send messages without speaking in that way made me feel he was Harpo Marx (without the horn and crazy wig). In this way, Andy showed me how the orb of energy could move with slight shifts in intention. We bounced around for a while, but eventually I got the gist of it. Inside our spaceship-like orb, I could see the energy fields of myself and Andy crossing each other, and at a certain point it felt like we were one being, with a strong sense of connectedness. I remember occasionally having this feeling in my earth body and wondered if at those times I was traversing a portal as well.

In this manner, Andy and I made several journeys together during which Andy was very insistent on showing me many different energies. I was shown many worlds that were different from any I'd ever been aware of, differences I could not only see but also feel and comprehend. Because of the way it was possible to use intention to maneuver the orb of energy, and because of seeing many different kinds of beings, I became aware of the fact that it doesn't matter what one's physical body looks like; what is important is the intention and the energy behind it. I saw beings scarier than Hollywood monsters, and yet their energy was gentle and loving; conversely, I also saw beings who were visually appealing but had hostile intentions. These journeys around the universe were a continuation of my training by Andy. Whenever Andy and I traveled together, he was often funny and animated, as if in this role of companion but also teacher he behaved closer to his true nature, even though he still looked like a dog.

One time Andy took us on what felt like a long journey, to a particular doorway that caused me anxiety. Even before we approached this particular doorway, I had a sense I didn't want to be there. I had the feeling that beyond this place my energy structure would dissipate completely. I sensed such fear and danger that I had trouble breathing. I had never felt this before, even when looking at very scary beings.

Andy hovered near, but not too close, to this doorway. I could not perceive anything on the other side, but there was no color at all. I looked at Andy, who was staring at the doorway, and for a moment I became even more frightened, because I thought he had somehow lost control of what was happening. But soon I realized that there was no doubt an important reason why Andy had deliberately brought me here. So I nudged Andy, who looked at me and then slowly back at the door, and as I followed his gaze, I could see forms moving around, ever so slightly peering at us, perhaps as curious to look at us as we were to look at them. Still I had a sense that if they came through that door, everything that I knew would change, and that the beings peering at us were probably thinking the same thing—grateful for whatever wisdom and intelligence keeps dimensions in their proper space. And yet we were not really separate, because we were relating emotionally, experiencing each other instinctively without needing to make contact in the physical dimension.

Because of this experience, I learned how to connect with the intentions of others, no matter how different they looked or felt, using a form of telepathy. Interestingly, on earth those who have such openness of perception are seen as intuitive, despite the fact that everyone is intuitive. In my dimension, everyone can feel the energy of others, and nothing is hidden, although this ability can still be better developed through practice. I remember reading somewhere, when I was still on earth, that the Australian Aborigines have the ability to feel telepathically, and they fear the human race would not survive if they should ever lose this ability. The ability to be telepathic is the measure of one's humanness and connection to all things.

My father has been trying to open back up into that lineage of telepathy to get to the core of who he is, just like every person on earth who feels disconnected or separated from spirit because some instinctual part of them has forgotten how to connect with others, the earth, and other dimensions.

Eventually in my travels with Andy I didn't need the orb of energy, because I learned how to control my emotions so I wouldn't run around like a kid in a toy store excited about experiencing so many diverse places and beings. Sometimes we would go down a path, other times we would travel down a river in a canoe. But always I knew the difference between being in a portal and being in my usual dimension surrounded by other beings who anchor this place, some of whom have an agreement to hold the matrix of this dimension together. I have been unable to discover who created these portals, or wormholes, between dimensions. You would think that when you arrive in heaven you would know everything instantly, but this is not the case. Continual learning and exploration are required to make ever new discoveries.

It was after one of these journeys that I made a particularly startling discovery. Feeling something had connected to my pants leg, I discovered a fuzzy ball that would change everything in my life, as well as many things in the lives of others—the being I would name Wyrme. After that, Wyrme joined me and Andy on many other journeys of exploration.

Editor's note: In reflecting on Galen's apparent fearlessness in traversing portals with Andy, I pondered what aspects limit our explorations in earth life and on the other side, and if fearlessness can be carried into different dimensions. This made me recall experiences of fearlessness in my childhood. When I was a young boy in primary school, my mother would sometimes visit a family friend who lived next to one of Los Angeles's flood-control channels. The channel was like a cement river with a bridge over it that had a steel guardrail. The sides were cement, but there was a little patch of dirt with some grass growing in one place about thirty or forty feet above the channel. On several occasions, I hopped over the guardrail and stood on this small patch of dirt and grass, without knowing if it was solid enough to prevent me from a very long fall. I suppose my attraction to the patch of dirt and grass was that it was the only natural part of that scene of concrete and iron so typical of Los Angeles. While it was a risk to stand on it, it wasn't being a risk-taker that made me do it so much as that it gave me a feeling of being exhilarated and supported while doing it.

I still remember how I was drawn to do it as if by a magnet. My conundrum is whether reason forged by my life experience actually protects me now or gets in my way. It seems we often have to make decisions between the mind and the heart.

I suppose one condition of being on the other side is that there we are able to pursue our curiosity and desires without fear of killing ourselves. And this may make us less fearful about exploring ourselves and our world in the next life or in other dimensions. It does seem as if qualities people have, such as fearlessness and love of adventure, are carried over to other dimensions, as Galen's actions seem to indicate. Galen has told me that because of the fearlessness I imparted to him, he doesn't have fear in his dimension and won't when he returns to earth.

CHAPTER 5

WYRME'S ARRIVAL

At the time the being I called Wyrme attached itself to me, Andy and I were using some traditional shaman-like visualizations for moving through portals, such as going down a river in a canoe. I had become better at holding my vibration, so I could travel without Andy's protective orb of energy around me and therefore was more exposed to the elements. I was wearing cargo pants with several pockets of various shapes and sizes that ran down my lower pants leg, and the brightly colored little fuzz ball was tucked behind one of these pockets where I could feel an added weight, but I had to pull the pants leg around before I found the creature. When I first saw it, I knew it was much more than just some portal fungus. Instead, it was a being with its own life force and energy. I gently touched it, and unlike a fuzzy caterpillar that might pull away from someone's touch, it moved toward my finger. I wasn't sure what to do with it, so I drew my hand back quickly. Andy gave me a look that conveyed the message that everything was fine but expressing puzzlement about how the creature could have gotten there.

"Do you think I should touch it again?" I asked Andy out loud. He gave a little whine that conveyed, "I would if I were you." So again I gently touched the top of the fuzzy ball, and a little lump came up. Like a caterpillar reaching from one leaf to another, it bobbed in the air a little before attaching itself to my open hand.

When it touched my hand, I felt calm and a sense that everything was okay. Then it pulled up its other half and completely moved into my palm, appearing to be about four or five inches long, and reared up. I was fascinated, but at the same time squeamish, feeling like I had been handed a large brown tarantula but with no idea what it was.

I studied it carefully and noted its flat, googly eyes, similar to ones on a child's toy. It had bands of intense color, only adding to its appearance as a plush toy. Sometimes its "head" with the googly eyes would arch up and stare back at me, although there never seemed to be anything looking out of those eyes.

After a few moments, it started to move way up my arm, and I was concerned about it getting near my face. But every time I started feeling anxious, I would soon feel something calming me, almost as if someone was giving me a "happy drug" to manage my anxiety. Meanwhile, Andy didn't seem concerned at all. He just watched the being move up my arm with the same fascination he would have had if he'd been observing a squirrel scampering up a tree.

Andy looked at Wyrme the same way any dog would look at something appealing, but he didn't jump up and try to grab Wyrme. I finally figured out that the fuzzy creature was protecting itself from Andy by generating an odor that only Andy could smell. I knew Andy wasn't a dog, and surely the creature knew this as well, yet there was something instinctive and animal-like about the behavior between the two of them.

When the creature got near my face and shoulders, it changed again, almost doubling its size, and started to vibrate and hum as if it was excited to have found a place where it could communicate. Later I learned that my shoulders were Wyrme's location of choice whenever it wanted to communicate with me. Its other favorite place became my chest, next to my beating heart (my body feels the same to me here as it did on earth). The being was a little more animated around my head and more rhythmic around my heart, but generally it matches whatever energy will best assist me emotionally.

When it got up around my head, I tried to look at it, but half of it was on one shoulder and half on the other, as if it were a fuzzy muffler. At that point, I had a feeling of being out in space. I experienced stars and nebula coming at me, as if I was moving through the cosmos, even though I did not feel any movement. Later, I would learn to travel with Wyrme in this way, but at that first encounter I felt it was showing me what it could do. Obviously, such sensations were familiar to Wyrme, though they were disconcerting to me. I wasn't losing my sense of reality, but the experience was making me dizzy. Eventually, Wyrme stopped, and Andy leaned up against my leg to anchor me.

Wyrme then carefully unwound itself from my neck and went to one side of my shoulders, where it vibrated, bringing me comfort. I suspect it had been testing me to see what kind of being I was and my limitations, and when it realized I wasn't able to do whatever it was trying to do at that moment, it stopped. It was then that I knew it had good intentions and was conscious enough to know my limitations—just like Andy—and that I could trust it.

Consequently, I gathered it back up in my hand and started petting it. Obviously, it liked to be touched, because it pushed up against my hand and fingers. And the more I sent it the positive energy of love and gratitude, the more it would respond by giving out different vibrations and creating various geometric patterns in its fur. Wyrme's surface could change almost instantly, just as an octopus's appearance is transformed by chromatophores in response to its environment.

I sat down on the grass because I was still a little dizzy, and I was going to set Wyrme down on the grass next to me to see if it would explore the grass in some way. But each time I tried to set it down, I would feel panic coming from it and its attempt to hold onto my hand. Clearly, Wyrme didn't want to be set down. Later, I learned that it preferred to be connected to something that had a conscious form and carried around like a pet. And I am embarrassed to admit that in the beginning that was what I thought Wyrme was—a pet. But the chaos Wyrme caused in the classroom when I took it with me to school one day made me dismiss the idea that it was a pet.

That day I took Wyrme with me to a lecture on intention with thirty students from earth, taught by a teacher named Binai, who stood more than eight feet tall and wore white flowing robes and a hood that covered most of his body, except for his translucent sea-green skin that revealed an underwater vista inside him.

Once in the classroom, Wyrme moved out of my pocket, expanded, plopped down to the floor, and glided in front of Binai. Then it projected thirty rainbow-colored fuzzy tentacles that moved toward the students and connected to each across their arms and shoulders, including myself. Everyone jumped out of their seats and attempted to pull the tentacles off. Binai stopped talking in midsentence to watch what was going on, then raised both arms and brought them together in a loud clap, creating a visible shock wave that distorted space, causing all the rainbow-colored tentacles to quickly retract and Wyrme to curl back into a small fuzz ball.

I was summoned to the study of my teacher, who asked, "Do you have any idea what you have here?"

I was told that Wyrme was just as good a name as any, because it was a rare and ancient being with no name, with unknown origins, that lives in the matrix of the universe but does not follow the laws of the universe. It was a being that could likely exist both in matter and antimatter and bridge polarity, but finds those who live with polarity a curiosity. There were only so many Wyrmes allowed to exist in the universe, and they scrupulously maintained those numbers, just like certain animals on earth that need a large territory will not crowd it if they have a choice.

I asked, "Have such creatures ever visited the earth?"

I was told these creatures were known to every plane of reality in our universe, but if they still came to earth, they remained small and inconspicuous. When they had visited earth's past, they were known as rainbow serpents by the Australian Aborigines, rainbow dragons by the Chinese, and Quetzalcoatl by Meso-Americans.

"Is it all right that I have Wyrme, then?" I asked the teacher.

The teacher warned, "This magical being has chosen to work with you and be your companion, and you seem to be balanced with it. It also seems to be learning a great deal from you. However, you need to be aware that it can take you places dimensionally that do not serve you. Be very clear with your communication and learn to say yes and no before you travel with it."

Sometimes in my dimension people don't focus on the big questions of why this and why that, but the arrival of this rare being became the catalyst for asking some profound questions. After speaking with my teacher, I was determined to learn more about these beings, as I suspected they had more purpose here than just meandering around. I thought perhaps they came at times of change or at other crucial times. Observing Wyrme as an example, I have noticed that although they do not heal others, they somehow find a unique vibration in the individuals they contact, with which to create peace, calm, and communication, suggesting these creatures are very conscious beings. They only seem to bring out and enhance qualities that are already in individuals, rather than adding or taking away, so everyone's experience with them is quite different.

Once I learned to travel with Wyrme, it became my constant companion, especially since it prefers not to be set down but to travel with a companion. At first, I wasn't sure what it was doing, but soon I realized that when I sat and it positioned itself on both shoulders, it was encouraging me to travel with it. Then, slowly, Wyrme would start expanding the space around my head, and I would see the stars and gases of the cosmos, until it located tunnels of swirling vapor that functioned as the "wormholes" Wyrme used for travel. That Wyrme used wormholes to travel was poetry that was not lost on me. Once I relaxed and began to travel with Wyrme, we became inseparable pursuing these activities.

Editor's note: when Galen first told me about his initial encounter with Wyrme, I wondered if the being had been drawn to him because of his childhood interest in magic worm tricks. At the head of the bed where I sleep is an aging Ziploc bag containing about fifty of the small magic trick worms with googly eyes I took from Galen's magic trick trunk when he first told me about Wyrme. Galen himself wondered if Wyrme appeared to him as a magic trick to convey the idea that it was not what it seemed to be, having searched Galen's memories of these magic trick worms and emulated them. The fact that Wyrme presents itself as a funny, stretchy, plush creature with googly eyes, both pleasant and silly, yet is also an incredibly powerful universe-altering being indicates that it is far more significant than its appearance suggests.

Wyrme's ability to act as a bridge to transdimensional travel intrigues me, especially when it attached itself to Galen and the being named Brock, allowing Galen to visit Brock's home planet and family in another dimension.[3] I asked Galen if it would be possible for Wyrme to do the same thing between Galen and me, even though an obvious difference was that I am not standing next to Galen as Brock was when Wyrme acted as a bridge that allowed Galen to travel to Brock's home planet. My interest in creating a Ken-Wyrme-Galen hookup was the possibility of having an interdimensional experience I could not achieve on my own.

Galen conveyed that this was a complex request, but that Wyrme was open to it. The logistical issue was that Wyrme *folds* space, not actually creating a bridge but instead bringing two points together, as when two dots on opposite ends of a piece of paper touch when the paper is folded. Connecting with me would require folding space in such a way that three points are connected—not impossible, I was told, but more difficult. All possibilities were being looked at in order to figure out how to accomplish this. Either Wyrme would come and find me, or the two of them would both come to me.

---

[3] From the chapter entitled "Earth Ambassador Brock" from *My Life After Life*.

Ultimately, the potential for success of this will depend on the laws of space and time, for linear time is the third point. The hookup needs to take place in my present, in linear earth time. Since time is a spiral, charting the most direct path from there to here could end up in a previous or future lifetime, so the challenge is for Wyrme to find me in an exact wrinkle in time where I exist on earth. While folding two points together is easy for Wyrme, the third point, the linear time point, will need to be somehow bent out from linear time, much like a two-dimensional dot on a piece of paper transmuting itself into three-dimensional space so it can rise up to meet the other two dots that are now folded together. This would have to be done in such a way that I would be conscious of the experience in my present. So it would require bending time while folding space.

To use a metaphor, I am asking Wyrme and Galen to find the movie reel that is me, not of just my present life but all past and all future lives my soul participates with on planet earth. Then I am asking them to find the one frame where Ken is conscious and connect with me in that moment.

***

I searched my memory to see if they had already attempted a hookup, but I aborted the attempt because it was in the wrong linear time sequence. There was only one unexplained event of a portal opening up in front of me. In the weeks prior to my attempt to visit Galen (and escape earth) through the Indigo Portal,[4] I would hear the fluttering of bird wings in my bedroom as if a large bird was ruffling its feathers. This happened at least twice, but I never saw anything, especially a large bird. Still, on earth Wyrme was known as the feathered serpent—at least on this part of the planet (southwestern North America). So, I am still left wondering…

[4] From the chapter entitled "There and Back Again" in *My Life After Life.*

CHAPTER 6

THE DARK BLOB

My discovery of Wyrme ultimately led to even more challenging adventurous journeys traversing portals and following wormholes to dimensions where I have been able to expand my knowledge of the universe and myself. On one particular evening, I felt a little amped up. I had experienced such high energy before, but usually when I began my evening of settling into a position where I can sleep, I can rest. Normally, one end of Wyrme rests on my shoulder, while the other end curls up on my chest, close to the beat of my heart. Having Wyrme on my chest, usually purring, is calming; it helps me to sleep and often go on excursions to visit other dimensions or people in dreams.

But on this occasion, I could not rest, and even Wyrme seemed amped up, in contrast to its usual tendency to enjoy going to bed to experience purring and connecting. I kept having the impulse to sit up, although I tried to fight it off, because I wanted to get some rest.

Nevertheless, I sat up in bed, with my feet on the floor, and Wyrme moved around my shoulders, its usual position for journeying. But this time it did not wrap itself around my neck; it hung down on my chest like a furry necklace. Suddenly, I felt like we were moving, accelerating at a great speed. I usually take such journeys with my eyes closed, but I kept my eyes open and saw that Wyrme looked very different, because it was arching out in front of me instead of relaxing on my chest. Also, our acceleration was greater than usual, the twists and turns through the wormholes more rapid, causing my senses to become a little disoriented.

Then abruptly Wyrme shifted into slow motion, and I wondered if I had looked like a smear of colors flying through the tunnels until the smear caught up with me. As we slowed down, Wyrme began to expand in diameter. Then it stopped in its tracks, seemingly on alert. I have seen Wyrme transform into a gray, puffy ball when it is disturbed with the world and pull away, but not this time.

I was a little fearful, as I could feel a different energy building in Wyrme and was not sure what it was up to. I knew Wyrme was more than just a fuzzy little pet, but I had not yet seen what it was capable of. It started expanding with a tremor, and all the pleasant, bright primary colors that made up its fur turned luminescent orange, like glowing embers. The now fiery Wyrme began to shift its position around me, keeping the right side of its tail end attached to the small of my back and the front half wrapped around so it was attached to itself over my heart. The section over my heart covered more area and was larger in diameter. I'd never seen Wyrme have an asymmetrical shape before. At the moment, I could hear something up ahead in the wormhole that sounded like rushing water. The louder the sound became, the more tightly Wyrme held me.

I now become quite frightened, as Wyrme began moving forward again—not as fast as when we had started off, but faster than I would have liked, going toward a sound that was unlike anything I had ever heard. If we came upon a curve in the tunnel, Wyrme slowed down the section of its body connected to me and allowed its front section to round the corner, as if checking for something before it pulled me around the curve.

Soon I began to feel pressure and smell a strong, putrid odor, wet and mildewy—a very stale smell as if it was coming from some kind of fungus. When Wyrme pulled me around the final curve, I was astonished to see ahead in the tunnel a large amorphous blue-black blob without eyes that contained some sort of writhing pupate thing inside that was apparently agitated upon seeing us. As it made the noise that sounded like rushing water, Wyrme responded by expanding its size. With both terror and fascination, I witnessed these two large creatures trying to out-maneuver each other. For a moment, I hoped the two creatures were simply trying to get each other to back off, but then the action escalated.

The dark blob growled, emitted more odor, and fired many black spores at us. Wyrme quickly detached itself from over my heart and, with the part of it attached to my sacrum, lifted me to safety behind it before engulfing the blob to absorb the spore it had expelled.

Wyrme was now in full battle mode, once again with all its familiar brilliant colors. Every part of Wyrme quivered like an upset porcupine, and its front section expanded out like the bell of a trumpet to pierce the blob and pull it apart from the inside out.

The blob crackled and expelled more pungent odor as it began to dissipate. Wyrme then punctured any remnants of the blob, tearing them apart until everything disintegrated. When it was clear that the blob had been obliterated, Wyrme collapsed in the tunnel with no energy or vibration coming from its seemingly lifeless body, even though it was still attached to my back, looking like someone had pulled off an oversized sock and thrown it on the floor.

Now I was alone in a wormhole somewhere in space, staring at what used to be Wyrme. A wave of terror and sadness hit me, and I began to cry. I arched back to stroke Wyrme where it was connected to my back, and as I did, I received a message—to calm myself and visualize Wyrme as I remembered it.

I made a great effort to close my eyes, meditated, and visualized Wyrme as I remembered it, while still touching Wyrme. Soon I began to feel Wyrme slowly expanding and then touching my chest. The next thing I knew Wyrme had positioned itself again on my shoulders, and I opened my eyes to find myself leaning up against my bed, right back where we had begun this journey. Wyrme immediately moved down from my shoulders and curled up around my neck, purring with happiness to be back in this space. The anxiety I had felt was now gone, and I only had a peaceful feeling.

I unwrapped Wyrme from my neck and held him in front of me to check his condition, but I found nothing on its body disturbed or lacking life force, nothing to verify what we had just gone through in the wormhole.

But I recalled everything that had taken place in that space, including the foul odor created by the dark blob, which I could still taste in my mouth. It was as if Wyrme had acted as a guard dog protecting me from harm, even though it was clearer than ever to me that Wyrme was nobody's pet.

In the morning, I sought out my teacher, because I needed to understand more about this encounter. By now, despite always cautioning me not to explore too much with Wyrme, my teacher knew very well that Wyrme and I had gone beyond what he had advised. When I reached my teacher, I explained what had happened in detail. It was the first time I had seen a look of concern on my teacher's face as his eyes opened a little wider and he raised his eyebrows. Then he sat down with a thoughtful look on his face and explained, "Sometimes, a malevolent energy from a malevolent universe will attempt to cross over into our benevolent universe, for the shadow is part of creation as well as the light. Wyrme can exist on both sides of this divide, and very likely can exist in an antimatter universe as well. And there are beings in the other universe that can also do that. Such creatures do not, as in a monster movie, come to our benevolent universe to destroy something; it's more like their very presence is harmful to everyone and everything in our benevolent universe. So it is not that they have bad intentions but that they operate in a different way, according to the rules of a different universe. When these beings come through, they destroy portals, tunnels, and any beings with which they come in contact. Anyone traveling in a tunnel who encounters them is exposed to something that forever alters them, if they survive, and makes it more difficult to remain in this universe with its benevolent ways. No doubt Wyrme, with its many levels of awareness and senses, knew that something malevolent had moved into a tunnel. One of the mysteries we have come to understand about this Wyrme being is that it protects this side of the universal divide, even though it could exist on the other side. I suspect that its affection for you and all it has come to know on this side prompted it to destroy that creature so that it could do no harm to anyone passing through that tunnel. I wonder if such creatures from different universes seek each other out, because I have heard of great battles between them where they have been seen tumbling through space." Then looking at me, my teacher added, "You are the one who has been chosen as Wyrme's traveling companion, so you were able to bring Wyrme back into its usual form."

"Was it dead?" I asked.

"No, it was not dead, and it would have come back eventually, but who knows how long that would have taken? You were available and a trusted source of love and energy capable of helping it, just as it assisted you during the encounter."

I was happy to hear that, but at the same time I was still not clear about what type of being Wyrme was. I asked, "Wyrme isn't a parasite, is it?"

"No, there is nothing parasitic about it. It chooses to fully engage with an individual's emotions, energy, and surroundings for a purpose. It doesn't hold back when it can serve." I thought about that for a moment, feeling guilty that I had wondered if I was being used by Wyrme.

Then my teacher, who has always been fascinated by Wyrme, asked me if he could touch it. The teacher held his hand out, and Wyrme, still connected to me, stretched over to my teacher's hand. As my teacher ran his fingers across its fur, certain patterns emerged on it in a way I had never seen when I had touched its fur. My teacher's face reflected wisdom, calmness, and clarity, and I sensed that he was exchanging messages with Wyrme. I saw his humanness, even though at the time I did not know whether my teacher was human. For the first time, I could feel a connection to my teacher I had never experienced before. I was grateful for that connection, because previously my teacher had always felt separate from me. Now Wyrme had brought us closer so we could interact in ways that would allow me to learn even more about the mysteries of the universe from him.

Editor's note: At the time of this experience, Galen did not yet know that his teacher was a member of the Angelic Kingdom, and while it is possible to feel great connectedness in the presence of such members, one never feels that one can relate to them as one might a friend. However, Wyrme was able to bridge the angel-human divide, allowing Galen to feel that his teacher was not so emotionally unreachable. Galen could then feel the teacher's emotions and relate them to his own experiences, allowing him, in turn, to be more open to the teacher's lessons.

In his travels with Wyrme, Galen was learning to appreciate the diversity of beings in the universe as well as its vastness. Although we do not need to know that there are multiple realities and multiple universes to function on earth, some of the richness of who we are is diminished, because this information isn't part of our normal thought processes. It is difficult to expand into true self-awareness if we do not know there is something to expand *into.*

As humans, we are trained to see with our eyes, and most of us *only* see with our eyes. But the illusions around us are hard to appreciate if our sight is limited to what comes through our eyes. Every so often someone may challenge preconceived notions about sight, such as a blind man who can paint anything in front of him with great detail. We are left to wonder if this occurs because the skin receives images and sends that input to the visual center of the brain (a connection that normally does not exist), or if it occurs as a result of telepathy, or both. In a sense, theoretical physicists see with their mathematics, and what they have seen of our reality tells them that it is but one of many dimensions, and our universe but one of many. But since there is no hard evidence of this that can be seen with the eyes, it is called *theoretical* physics. But it would not be difficult to imagine that our universe, with its uncountable galaxies and stars, is but one of many bubbles in a giant cosmic bubble bath. Such a vision should not make us feel insignificant in the face of such an unfathomable creation, but perhaps it should serve as a catalyst in the expansion of our consciousness.

One day science will be less timid about sharing some of these secrets with the rest of us, and when they are finally shared, it is my hope they will make our lives richer and help us cherish even more the little blue marble we call earth.

CHAPTER 7

BRIDGES BETWEEN BEINGS

The experience with the dark blob shook me up. Until now, I had always felt safe in my environment, as if everything in my new dimension was contained and I was living in a fishbowl. There was a predictability about everything here being energy or intention, and knowing how to create from this knowledge. I had grown accustomed to a certain rhythm in my daily activities, such as hanging with friends, being with Wyrme or Andy, and meeting different individuals with unique stories. But I had never before been exposed directly to something so very different from this happy, safe place, and for a while it was disturbing that there was something else out there counter to what was being created where I am.

This realization caused me to ponder what fear does to us, even in this dimension, which is considered heaven— a place where people think fear shouldn't exist. For me, my primordial need to be vigilant for survival as a human now turned into fear of the unknown.

As a result, I had to work with my new sense of loss of control and safety for a while. I thought about how Wyrme, knowing it was needed to protect a wormhole, responded without fear. Wyrme didn't take me to battle with the blob as insurance or because I just happened to be its traveling companion. This journey clearly had provided me with a tremendous opportunity for learning about courage in the face of fear. Reflecting on the fearlessness Wyrme had displayed while traveling with me through the wormhole and protecting me from the dark blob inspired me and made me wonder if any of the creatures like Wyrme had ever been killed by anything, because they seemed like such present, clear, and fearless guardians of the universe. And yet they are the silliest-looking things imaginable, reminding me again that things aren't always as they appear. Consequently, I began to imagine what it would be like to live fearlessly and be open to the energy of what *is* rather than fear of what *might be*. I thought although there might be big stinky dark blobs out there destroying tunnels and shooting spores at people, in this moment and space they are not here.

To further ponder this experience with Wyrme, often I retreated to my favorite rock and stared into the sky, looking for The Great I. But other times I lay in bed until I drifted off to sleep, going on journeys in dreams. Eventually, I concluded that I did not need to fear that such things as the dark blob were going to come crashing through the sky down on the landscape like meteors. I felt safe and connected again, especially with Wyrme curled up on my chest and purring and Andy also lying on my bed.

It was during one such peaceful rest state that I felt Wyrme move. I thought perhaps it was readjusting itself, but when I opened my eyes, I saw it extending itself over to Andy, not touching him, but hovering over his heart, then his throat, and a few other places, as if they were having a conversation. During this process, Andy had a look of wisdom and intelligence in his eyes. I heard no sound from either one, only Andy's breathing subtly changing and Wyrme's vibration, which I could feel because it was still attached to my chest.

Andy seemed to be in a trancelike state, which I have also experienced with Wyrme. Finally, Andy looked at me, and I could tell his trance was over because his breathing became normal. But Wyrme was still extended, which Andy took advantage of by licking the end of Wyrme hovering near him. Wyrme recoiled immediately from what appeared to be a kiss as if it was disgusted, and then they both ignored each other again.

"Okay, what is going on?" I asked the two of them, although I didn't expect a revealing conversation. Neither one reacted to my question. I examined Andy to see if Wyrme had left an energetic imprint, but Andy seemed like his usual self. Then I brought Wyrme over to Andy, who sniffed at it, sneezed, and lay down as if he wasn't interested. Now they didn't act the least bit interested in each other.

For the next several days, I tried unsuccessfully to catch them behaving this way again, which was irrational because Wyrme always knew if I was awake or asleep. I became frustrated, feeling like they were keeping a secret from me. I didn't want anything to disturb the bubble of happiness and safety I was trying to reestablish, and I found this mystery upsetting. After a week, I finally surmised that whatever was going on between Wyrme and Andy must be the same sort of connection Wyrme had with me, although I found it interesting that Wyrme made no attempt to touch Andy in any way. All attempts to have Andy and Wyrme touch were always met with resistance, and I was curious enough about the reason for this to ask my teacher for an explanation. But even more, I wanted to know about what I had been feeling after the encounter with the dark blob.

My teacher welcomed me into his home, invited me to sit in a chair, and said, "Ah, you have been thinking."

"Yes, I have been thinking," I responded.

I explained my thoughts and feelings concerning my new sense of fear in this place where I was growing and gaining more understanding. I told him how I liked the school-like aspect of this dimension, yet the fear of not feeling safe anymore was disrupting my world. I also told him about waking up to find Wyrme and Andy having some sort of strange communication, which had been unsettling to me.

My teacher perked up upon hearing that Andy and Wyrme had been conversing, and I realized in a flash that their actions had not been about leaving me out of a conversation, because I couldn't be in on Wyrme's conversations any more than I could have been in on the conversation Wyrme had had with my teacher. Instead, I began to appreciate even more how Wyrme was able to be a bridge not only between dimensions but also between beings.

At that point, Wyrme began to emerge from my pocket and stretch toward the teacher, who opened his hand. When I saw the delight on my teacher's face as Wyrme moved its whole body into his hands, I felt a fleeting fear that Wyrme could leave me. It wasn't jealousy, but more because I had come to pride myself, particularly after the tunnel incident, that Wyrme *needed* me. But soon I realized that was the point. I was a free being on my own journey, and it didn't always involve what Wyrme was doing or feeling. In that moment, I knew I had to let go of feeling so connected to Wyrme, because Wyrme belonged to no one. Then I was able to laugh to myself watching my teacher petting Wyrme and talking to it, glad to see again a warmer side of my teacher.

My teacher then told me again that Wyrme is a bridge, and that it is so curious that its very nature is a desire to gain knowledge and understanding. Once it gains such knowledge, it can assist others, and it always will if it knows it can help, having great insight about what it can and cannot do.

Then my teacher explained more specifically, "I cannot tell you what the communication between Andy and Wyrme was about, but my sense is that Wyrme is preparing Andy for something, just as it prepared you to travel and open your consciousness."

I wondered what Andy could prepare for. Although I knew he was not just a dog, he always played his role so beautifully that sometimes I didn't think of him as anything but a happy dog. Instead, I had to try to see everything as it *is*, rather than how I assumed it to be. When I took this new perspective into account, I suddenly saw a radiance around my teacher that I had never seen before. I realized that I had often assumed too much rather than truly seeing with clarity, but in this one moment I managed to break that pattern.

Finally, I decided not to worry about what Wyrme was preparing Andy for, as that was between Andy and Wyrme. Instead, I vowed to remain in the present so I could continue my path of learning and understanding.

As if my teacher had understood what I had just come to appreciate, he smiled at me and, as he handed Wyrme to me, said, "Here, I think I need to hand this back to you. Thank you. Do you have any other questions, Galen?"

"No, I think it is pretty clear now what I have been working through," I answered.

Editor's note: For many who believe in an afterlife, there is a sense that after we leave the physical body, we are separate from the experiences we had before leaving. But Galen's actions show that there is a very human side to being in this other place, reflected in how Galen worked with some very human feelings about fear and security after his experiences with the dark blob and Wyrme communicating with Andy.

Heaven has always been an exclusive place—if we are good enough, we will go there—or a place of transformation, where beings are perfected. But this is an illusion, as demonstrated by Galen's efforts in processing and learning from some of his tendencies and experiences. Galen has also pointed out that nothing is stopping us from doing our inner work now, on earth, before we pass over to the other dimension. The only advantage of processing in Galen's dimension is that the personality is much more neutral. and polarity isn't operational, and therefore it is not such a distraction. But that does not mean we should postpone for tomorrow in another dimension what we should be doing today in this dimension of earth.

Even though earth is an inherently unsafe place, with dangers ranging from avalanches, stampeding zebras, or living downwind from a nuclear reactor, and while any day could be our last on earth, it isn't healthy to always think about this, because that doesn't allow us to be fully present in the moment and learn from our experiences, which is why we are here, regardless of how ephemeral our sojourn on this planet may be. Safety is about *being*, as in being a conscious member of this universe, but not about being where we are at any particular moment. We have free will and the choice to worry about potential dangers, but that seems to be a road that leads nowhere except to anxiety.

Unfortunately, many individuals hold back in their lives on earth, waiting to get to heaven so they can really live, but Galen shows that we can live and learn anywhere, as long as we are paying attention and present. Galen has had the opportunity to meet many people in his new dimension that he would never have had the chance to meet during his limited earth experience. When we understand how spirit and energy flow, then everything has beauty. Being alive on earth is not about preparing oneself to go somewhere else at death. It is about being in the moment, being compassionate and open to the experience that we are participating in the here and now.

The reason people incarnate is to create experience, and for those who choose to incarnate—those souls who want to learn and grow through this modality—incarnate life continues, and not always on earth.

So if having valuable experiences is what is important, it would behoove us to appreciate that it isn't about where we are going but where we are now, and how much effort we make to participate with the opportunities at hand. When the day comes that we are in another time and place, we will be using the same skills we are working with now. And if we have chosen to be disconnected and non-participatory here on earth, that will be the skill set we bring with us. Galen told me that no matter what dimension we live in, there is a here and now, and growth is about the experiences we have. Experiences exist to serve us, no matter what form or dimension we are in. And the more awareness we bring to our experiences, the more they teach us.

CHAPTER 8

THE SHIMMERING

One morning I woke up and again felt drawn to go to school, something I had not felt for some time. On earth such a long absence from school would have been considered very bad, but here people attend class only when prompted. After getting dressed, I walked to the familiar hallways and peeked into each classroom to sense what energies were developing that might spark my interest.

From its external appearance, you would think this school is massive, but up to this point I had never seen more than a handful of classrooms. Although the classrooms can change and be very different from each other, usually only recognizable by where a blackboard or lectern is positioned, there was something in each classroom that functioned as a visual anchor for me, so I had a sense of whether I'd been in them before.

Eventually, I was drawn into a room and sat down in a seat, happy that I was going to learn something new. The first thing I noticed was that all the students in the classroom with me appeared to be girls or young women. I double-checked with myself to make sure I was in the right room, thinking I might be in a girl's health class, but concluded that this was where I needed to be according to my intuition and inner feelings.

Soon a very beautiful, etheric teacher came into the room. I was fascinated by how her indistinct, transparent, misty appearance made it seem like a strong wind could disperse her.

The teacher announced that this class was about finding one's comfort zone concerning feminine energy and qualities, such as nurturing. The teacher explained that even though on earth masculine and feminine energy are seen as polarized, in the universe they are parts of a continuum of energy. Feminine energy is a connecting energy that permeates everything but is not separate from anything. It gives energy the means to manifest and change its form. Chaos is simply formless energy seeking form, and it is feminine energy that allows energy to assume form. Normally, when I consider feminine energy, I think it is about being sensitive, delicate, or even submissive, but despite the teacher's delicate appearance, nothing about her was submissive. She taught the subject with utmost authority.

As I looked into her eyes, I was able to travel inwardly to that familiar space where I felt connected to everything. I also experienced and felt a deep desire to be flexible and creative. As I came back to my own space, I concluded that I needed to better understand this level of connection to everything, which differs from the feeling in meditation or when Wyrme touches me. From this lesson I learned that feminine energy helps people use the energy of connection to create at a very fundamental level.

After the teacher had left and I looked around the room again, I noticed the students were not all female after all. There was a mixture of the sexes and even some non-humans. Apparently, the teacher had wanted everyone in the class to have a feminine form to challenge students concerning our perceptions about the polarity of masculine and feminine energy, so we would learn that such energy is not separate but is part of a continuum.

And I had to admit that I had felt a sense of separateness in the class between myself and what I had perceived were female classmates, as well as between my notions of feminine and masculine energy. After class I was able to better see the illusion of this polarity.

While heading home, I decided to stop by my favorite rock. As I was looking out over the horizon, I observed a patch of shimmering in the landscape, looking like a wavy mirage one might see in a desert or rising off hot pavement. In this patch of shimmering light I could make out the images of three people walking toward me from very far away. When I rubbed my eyes and blinked, the shimmering light was gone. I decided I had stared at the teacher so long in class that some of her energy was affecting my vision, and I fell asleep.

When I woke up, I felt a little like Rip Van Winkle, because it seemed I had napped so long that the atmosphere felt different.

Heading home, I passed some people sitting near a grove of trees, and I studied them to see if I recognized any of them. Then I saw a patch of shimmering light nearby, this time containing images of a larger group of individuals. The light seemed to be moving across the ground toward the group talking near the trees. I felt a sense of urgency to say something, because I was still a little on edge after encountering the dark blob and wasn't sure if the shimmering light could be dangerous.

With Andy barking at my side, I ran over to the trees where the group was sitting and cautioned them, "Can you see what's coming toward you? Get out of the way." They looked at me like I had lost my mind, because the light had vanished, and replied, "There is nothing dangerous here. What are you afraid of?"

I felt embarrassed and said, "Oh, I thought I saw something."

I had no doubt that I had seen something, but it could have been caused by something from my last class. I thought for a minute about going to my teacher, but I was unsure about myself and decided to just go home instead.

When I woke up the next morning, my concerns about the patch of shimmering light were gone, and I chalked the experience up to having been overtired. But as I opened my front door, on the horizon across the hill below my house there was a whole band of shimmering energy in which I saw people. My reaction was to back up and shut the door, which I have to admit is funny, because if this energy band was coming to get me, shutting my front door was not going to stop it.

As soon as I had summoned more courage, I decided to go find out what it was. As I came closer to it, I just closed my eyes and walked right into it. Inside the band of shimmering light, I felt invigorated, like I had been given a dose of the best vitamins in the world. Andy was by my side, but Wyrme, who had been attached to me, was nowhere to be found. I checked my pockets, felt around my neck, and looked on the ground in case I had dropped it. I decided to leave the band of shimmering light to look for Wyrme, and once outside it Wyrme was visible on my chest. Fascinated, I stepped back into the band of shimmering light, and Wyrme became again invisible—and then back out, and Wyrme was there again.

I was pondering why this was happening to Wyrme when the band of shimmering energy became larger and moved forward toward my house. I found a path where I could avoid it and went to my teacher to get an explanation of what was happening.

When I reached my teacher, he described the phenomenon and my fear of it.

He said, "There is nothing wrong. What you are calling a band of shimmering light is a magnetized energy force that appears occasionally to purify and revitalize the energy field here when it has been affected by many thoughts and visions."

I was astonished at the beneficial nature of this phenomenon, which explained why I had felt invigorated inside the shimmering energy. But I still didn't understand how it could make Wyrme invisible. So, I said, "I walked into the band of light with Andy and Wyrme, but Wyrme was invisible inside it."

My teacher looked at Wyrme and me as he pondered for a minute. Then he affectionately touched Wyrme and answered, "There are many things we don't understand about this holographic being that can live in almost any environment. It is still a mystery even to those of us who are teachers and have seen many things. We have never had such a creature in this dimension when one of these purifications is occurring, but I suspect that the energy force that revitalizes the energy field here shares the same frequency on which Wyrme operates, or combines with its energy in a way that causes Wyrme to become invisible."

He then asked me if I could feel Wyrme's weight after it became invisible, but it was more like I still felt Wyrme's presence more than its weight.

I suggested an experiment to see if we could determine more. My teacher and I went to one of the shimmering bands of light slowly moving across the landscape, and I walked to the side of it, extending my hand holding Wyrme into the light. While my arm looked slightly distorted, Wyrme's image was not distorted, yet all I could make out was a faint outline of its body. I pulled my arm out, and as my teacher touched Wyrme, his fingers entered its body. As he removed his fingers from Wyrme, some of its colorful fuzz adhered to his fingers, as if Wyrme's body had become a different kind of material. Almost immediately Wyrme became solid again, with its usual display of patterns and colors. I excitedly put Wyrme into the shimmering light again, left it in there for a few seconds, pulled it back out, and touched it, but my fingers did not enter its body, perplexing me.

My teacher reported that for a second he had been able to detect Wyrme's desire to merge with him in that space. I theorized that perhaps Wyrme had a different response to me because, unlike my teacher, I am not an angel. Hoping to learn more, I asked my teacher, "Do you have a desire to merge with Wyrme?"

"Yes, I suppose I do, for I feel very connected to it with all its curiosity and rarity."

So apparently Wyrme, true to its nature, had been responding to an external desire of my teacher. It seemed to me that something almost miraculous had taken place when three different entities had gathered together, perhaps for the first time in the universe—a human boy from earth, an angel, and Wyrme. The experience of the band of purifying shimmering light and Wyrme's invisibility in it taught me a great deal about how everything in the universe is designed to work together in various combinations.

After the band of shimmering light had finished purifying the energy field, the difference in the environment could be easily felt. All my senses were heightened, everything felt so alive that the grass crackled beneath my feel as I walked, and it seemed everyone's awareness had increased. Colors were more vivid and sounds more intense. It reminded me of how vital and vivid everything had seemed when I first arrived here—because everything was new and fresh—despite the confusion I experienced from having crossed over.

Editor's Note: When I asked Galen why he perceived only a handful of classrooms in a school building that seemed so majestic from the exterior, he said that he later realized that the school is actually very expansive, with many classrooms, but at the time he related this story he was still growing into his new dimension, and he perceived the school as small as a way to make it seem manageable and help focus in the classrooms. When one first enters Galen's dimension, it is possible to be overwhelmed by the sheer variety and scope of things that make it hard to participate in all potential experiences in a focused manner. So sometimes perceptions are limited to allow the newly arrived to experience things in a less overwhelming, more focused way that facilitates participation with soul and spirit.

Controlling or limiting his perceptions initially helped Galen to better focus on and understand his new dimension. Galen said it is like being a monk who can focus in on what a particular energy is teaching without being distracted by other energies. Even on earth we filter out information that doesn't serve us. So there is logic to the orientation that occurs in Galen's dimension, which assists individuals on their paths.

Further, Galen's exhilarating experience with the purifying band of light not only taught him about how the various elements of the universe are designed to work together, but it gave him an example of how energy and life are periodically renewed in various dimensions, and that what may appear first as a destructive force can actually be a purifying force.

CHAPTER 9

PURSUIT OF THE SELF

During the purification period I spent a lot of time outdoors, because it felt so invigorating to be in nature. One day I was sitting with Andy and Wyrme at my rock when I heard a new sound similar to the mocking laughter of munchkins giggling at Dorothy from behind the bushes when she arrived in the Land of Oz.

It had a fake quality, as if it were being produced on a Hollywood soundstage. The more I heard it, the more it irritated me. But when I turned to see what was causing it, I couldn't find its origin.

It was hard for me to ignore it, as it limited my enjoyment of the revitalized energy in the environment and kept drawing my attention, as if it was pursuing me. The only place it would not bother me was in my house or other buildings, but I didn't want to stay indoors and miss the intensified beauty of nature following the recent energy purification. Eventually, I became obsessed with identifying what it was so I could somehow stop or avoid it. When I attempted to resolve this mystery by searching for its cause, out of the corner of my eye I would see something moving, like a figure darting behind some object. But when I'd go to the spot where I'd seen it, there would be nothing there.

Its very nature was aggravating to me, which was unusual, because I was rarely aggravated in this dimension, even though I was sometimes pensive or sad.

It seemed to be playing a game with me, while Andy and Wyrme were just ignoring it. I didn't know whether to keep trying to catch it or just try harder to ignore it.

One day when I woke up knowing it was a school day, I realized that I would have to run the gauntlet of this taunting sound to get to school, but that it would not follow me into the building and distract me.

While walking to school I detected a figure walking parallel with me. On the count of three, I whirled around to look at it, and standing right in front of me was a figure looking exactly like myself, the same height, with the same eye and hair color, and wearing the same outfit.

Surprised, I took a step back, and it also took a step back. I raised my right hand, and it raised the same hand. The figure seemed to mimic all my movements, but it did not have a dog like Andy or a creature like Wyrme. An interesting mix of emotions rose up in me, a blend of competitiveness, anger, and frustration. I turned to walk away from it, hoping it would disappear, but instead it walked away in the opposite direction, at the same pace and with the same number of steps. There was nothing

I could do without it mimicking my movement, to the point where I felt this being, whatever it was, was haunting and mocking me.

So I quickened my pace, believing that once at school it would not follow me indoors just as the mocking voice did not. And indeed, the minute I walked through the door, I turned around and it was gone.

The minute I entered the classroom, all my obsessive thoughts about the figure left me and I regained my usual pleasant emotional state. The teacher looked normal, everything in the class was predictable, and the lesson involved nothing very challenging—for which I was grateful. But when class was over, I began to feel anxious again about the figure awaiting me. I stood for a while just inside the entrance to the school, wondering if I should ask my teacher about this situation, recalling that when I first met him, he had also looked like me, which was my teacher's way of creating a sense of comfort and familiarity for me. But this situation seemed different.

I decided not to go to my teacher because I just wanted to try and get rid of this clone without a big fuss. And when I found it was still my constant companion once I was outdoors, I decided to confront it.

"I give up," I yelled out loud to the figure, and it yelled the same words right back at me. And when I laughed, it laughed, too. I didn't know what else to do, so I just went home, knowing once I was inside it would not follow me.

When bedtime came, I went to sleep comforted by Wyrme, who was in his usual position around my neck and chest, and Andy, who was beside the bed. I experienced a deep satisfaction at everything being in its proper place, and I fell asleep. But then I had a dream in which the mocking voice appeared, which does not happen often to me in this dimension where processing is ongoing. In the dream I was floating above the seashore and could hear the mocking voice in the background. I decided to take care of this thing once and for all, so I descended to the barren beach full of small stones. I turned around to look in the direction from which the voice had been coming, and standing in front of me was a mirror image of myself. However, this time it wasn't dressed like me. Instead, it was wearing padded body armor, including a breastplate and a helmet that revealed half the face. Since the figure was dressed for combat, I quickly grabbed some micalike flat, jagged stones for defense. Then I assumed a fencer's stance, challenging the figure, even though it had no weapon.

We began to spar, and I took a few jabs at it, but it anticipated my every move. I changed my tactic, and instead of advancing with one step forward and then lunging, I advanced with two steps, hoping to surprise it, which I did. Then, with two thrusts, I pierced the figure in the chest. As I did this, the long stone turned into a piece of mirror and fell to the ground and broke. I could now see the image of the figure that had been mocking me reflected in all the pieces of the mirror now on the ground. As my heart sank, fearing I had created more of the mocking figures, I woke up. As I lay awake for a while trying to interpret what my dream was trying to tell me, I began to understand that the figure mocking me probably was an aspect of myself. But I still wasn't sure what it was trying to communicate.

In the morning when I opened my door to leave for school, there was the figure again, looking eager to share the day with me. But now it no longer gave me the same level of discomfort as before. I was even able to say good morning to it as I walked toward school. And my changed attitude seemed to affect its energy, making it less excited than I'd become accustomed to. I realized that my own agitation and frustration had caused *it* to mirror these emotional qualities, too.

I headed for a lecture on universal laws concerning how the soul communicates with its own aspects, or parts of it that manifest as a personality, using images of those aspects. In the class, I was reminded of how I knew that here everything is expressed as a symbol or an archetype and functions to provide insights. This is the beauty of my dimension, although similar things occur on earth to provide insights if people are paying attention. We receive exactly the information we need for our understanding. Realizing this, I now believed with more certainty that the figure that had been mocking me was not some kind of unwanted visitor who had slipped through a wormhole to wreak havoc in my environment, but actually an aspect of myself that I had not yet looked at or worked with. After class, pleased with my theory, I went to my teacher for confirmation of my view. He explained, "The energy force that came through to purify the energy field created a renewed opportunity to work with various aspects of the self and gain a deeper understanding. You just happened to manifest this on a very physical level."

"That is what my dream and the lecture showed me, that it was a reflection of myself. But how did this come about?" I responded.

"Because the energy is supportive of manifesting things in a way that serves the highest good for the individual, it created a physical form. It took a while for it to fully manifest, which is why you couldn't see it fully at first, but later, after it had fully manifested, you could confront it," my teacher answered.

My teacher then talked to me about how valuable it is to see aspects of oneself in everything, because of an understanding that all things are actually connected. In my dimension, universal laws are clearer than on earth because there is no polarity here, but on earth the laws are just as true. Seeing a part of yourself in everything around you teaches you not only to relate to everything but also how to relate to *yourself*.

I remember that on earth I had doubts about aspects of myself, parts that I felt were inauthentic and perhaps irritating to others. I experienced anger about not being able to get away from certain thoughts and situations that felt surreal to me. However, I did not gain insight into any of this until recently, when I realized that ignoring such feelings did not make them go away. This could only be done by facing the aspects of myself.

As I listened to my teacher talk about the value of confronting aspects of ourselves, I began to see how the things that rise up in front of us are having a conversation with us—reminding us of unfinished work or our relationships with everything around us. I knew the aspects now facing me had come from my earth life, and I said, "Well, I thought I had cleared all that!"

My teacher answered, "We just went through a purifying cycle, and now everyone in this dimension is going through a personal purifying cycle. Soul and source energy always send waves of purifying energy to align everything with the original intention of unified energy. Even though you think you might have cleared up this or that, or that something wouldn't ever be a problem again, there is always residue that can be further clarified and aligned."

At this point, I could see with greater clarity what I had carried around with me during my earth life and how and why it had come back to haunt me in this dimension—to teach me. But I had responded at first to it the same way I had on earth—by judging myself and others—and this tendency had undermined my understanding and peace of mind. The conversation with my teacher had showed me how to view confronting aspects of the self differently, as a further opportunity for comprehending myself and my potential in this new dimension.

After I left my teacher and went back out into the world, I could hear the mocking voice again, but now it seemed more like that voice of a happy child that faded into the afternoon.

Editor's note: I pointed out to Galen how similar his dream was to the scene in the movie *Star Wars: The Empire Strikes Back*, where Yoda has Luke Skywalker go into a cave and confront Darth Vader, and they do battle with their light sabers. Luke wins the fight and pulls the mask off the destroyed Darth Vader, only to find his own face behind the mask.

All humans, whether in the best or worst of circumstances, have questions or doubts about aspects of their personalities. The struggle with our self-images is the work of what I call "The Dweller." In this regard, Galen was no different. He told me that he was never entirely comfortable in his own skin because he felt a part of him both mocked others and felt mocked. So he often felt "fake."

Just as the observer self is the most refined aspect of our personalities, "The Dweller" is the most unrefined aspect—our shadow self or that part of the ego that undermines us and prevents us from being at peace with ourselves. It is very rare for individuals to feel completely at peace with themselves all the time, especially in our society and at this time on earth. Daily we are bombarded with information that causes self-doubt about almost every aspect of ourselves, except perhaps in our own homes.

Aspects of us function as mirrors to show us truths about parts of ourselves and our interactions with others, a function illustrated in Galen's dream when he sparred with his double using the weapon of a stone that is then transformed into mirror shards as it fell to the ground. It is enlightening to work with these reflections, as they not only show us our faults, but also sometimes our most powerful traits—ones we can utilize to better advantage in the future. Life is all about a dance of these parts of ourselves that want our attention so they can help us gain increased understanding about our lives.

Using introspection to comprehend various aspects of ourselves gives us a great deal of insight and the possibility of alignment with spirit, but this can be a challenge in our fast-paced lives on earth. Introspection is to the mind what a cleansing shower is to the body.

CHAPTER 10

AGREEMENT WITH GLEN

My day-to-day routine of going to school, meeting new people, walking around with Andy and Wyrme as companions, and traveling wherever I want has made life here wonderful. This dimension is "heaven," because it provides experiences above and beyond what can be experienced on earth, and yet most of what I experience here is still available on earth, even though it may have to be approached differently.

On one particular day, I had the desire to spend time among very large trees, like the giant redwood forests with which I was familiar on earth and considered magical. I have learned that if I want to experience something here, all I have to do is open my front door, walk down the path leading to my house, and imagine what I choose to manifest. During such times, Wyrme is in sync with what I create, just as I am in sync with what Wyrme creates for me to experience. Wyrme is usually either in my pocket or hanging around my neck, and it emits rhythmic pulses that sound like purring when it is pleased with certain experiences. I am not completely sure why Wyrme chose me to be its vehicle, but it may be because it likes to participate in my experiences, even though Wyrme has likely been to every corner of the universe and surely various places on earth as well.

After leaving my house on this day, according to my desire I walked on a beautiful trail among giant trees, watching the light filter through their branches. Soon I came to a place overlooking a stream and sat down beside it. Since I had created the woods and stream through my intention and desire, I was surprised to hear someone else walking in this environment. I looked over my shoulder and saw a young man about my age walking toward me. I nodded and said, "Hello," and he nodded and returned the greeting.

"If you like, have a seat. I was just taking a walk and enjoying the water. You are welcome to join us. My name is Galen, and this is Andy," I offered.

After noticing he was looking at my shoulder, where Wyrme was sitting, I added, "Oh, and this is Wyrme."

The young man sat down and said, "My name is Glen. I like the redwoods myself, and often I come just to enjoy the trees. I try to visit as often as I can right now."

I thought it was interesting that he said, "right now," because here people can go anywhere at any desired time, as they have unlimited freedom of movement outside of the constraints of linear time.

Glen and I remained silent for a while, just listening to the stream. Then he looked over at Wyrme, who had come around from the back of my neck to my chest and was checking Glen out, as I could see from the changes of colors and patterns in its fur, looking like the light flicker on banks of computers in a sci-fi movie.

Wyrme seemed more curious than usual about Glen, at one point even extending one end of itself toward Glen, who wasn't sure what to do about it.

"Just hold your hand out," I said to Glen.

Glen cautiously opened his hand, and Wyrme settled in his palm for a while. Then it drew itself back and reconnected to me.

Glen said, "That creature gave me an odd feeling—both cool and warm and vibrating all at the same time."

I filled Glen in on what I knew about Wyrme and how it had come to be with me. Then Glen said, "Thank you. I am trying to experience as many things as possible right now while I can."

After hearing this I noticed a subtle light blue aura around Glen, so I knew he was preparing to go back to earth.

"I am getting ready to go back to earth," Glen stated flatly, confirming my assumption.

"Are you happy about that?" I asked.

"Yes, I'm excited about it, but there is a part of me that is going to miss this place, where you don't have to think all the time about what you are doing, or what you are experiencing; you just do things instinctually."

"I do understand that," I replied. "But it is really not that different on earth. Sure, you have to work with things a little differently, and when you go back you have to forget."

Glen nodded, then said, "I have had a series of experiences where I went back to earth for a short time, then came back here. The last three such trips have been very short, and as a result this body is only age twenty-two."

Puzzled by this revelation, I asked, "Why were you there for such a short time?"

Glen continued, "I used up all my energy in a very short time, sort of like a shooting star. So for the last several times I've returned I agreed to have a shorter life in exchange for a connection to some incredible people who were caring for me or were my teachers. And the wisdom and the opportunity I gained from that now allows me to be a teacher for some of these amazing people. So, I have made agreements to have shorter lives with more impact, rather than a longer life with slow growth over time. I have become very used to this kind of arrangement, but this time I am going to agree to have a longer life, so I am not going to experience the specialness that I did in other lives. Still, I will have some memory and some understanding available to me."

I found it interesting that Glen remembered all these past journeys to earth, perhaps because they occurred so close together.

Glen went on, "It was my agreement in these past lives to recall a lot about who I was, so I have been very conscious throughout. This made birth a little wild. I had awareness of things before I could even see them or connect to them. But during my past three lives I have had some sort of disability, so as part of my agreement to have a very conscious existence, I have never been able to communicate well."

After Glen described how he passed out of these lives quickly, he added, "This time I do not know how I will navigate through a long life. I may not remember as much, and my experiences may slow down a lot more. I am nervous because I do not know what to expect."

"Will there be people there that you know?" I asked.

"Oh yes, I am gathering my list now," Glen replied.

I found this an interesting statement, as I had never known it was possible to create a list of favorite connections.

Then Glen surprised me by saying, "I would like you to be on my list. That is why I came here to seek you out, so that I could meet you again at some point in the future."

I was stunned and didn't know how to answer, so I asked, "What would I do? Who would I be?"

"There are several options. Has your teacher talked to you yet?" Glen asked.

I said, "No. I could agree to come back very quickly if I could be my father's child again, but my teacher has not mentioned such an opportunity. Glen, what role would I have in your life?"

"Well, I can't reveal too much to you, but we can agree to meet and recognize each other. If that is enough to make an agreement, then I would not interfere with your choices in determining when you come back to the earth plane and what relationships you have there. You would have free will and choice, of course."

I thought about this and said, "I don't see any reason why I can't agree if this is not going to change my timeline or affect my free will."

Glen reassured me, "Making such an agreement won't change your timeline."

"Then I will agree. In whatever capacity, whenever we come together, I will agree to recognize you. I will agree that we sat here in front of this stream by this redwood forest and had this conversation about life on earth." I felt like I should do something else, so I shook his hand, and we smiled at each other. Just making such an agreement made me curious about my next life on earth and what connections and level of consciousness I might have then.

After we made this agreement, Glen went back down the same path he had come up. I sat by the stream for a while, continuing to consider how unusual this experience with Glen had been and what my next earth life would be like.

Since I am completely happy where I am right now, and have opportunities for so many different experiences here, it also made me a little nervous to think about making any changes.

When I got back to my house and thought about this more, I realized that I didn't fully understand my agreement with Glen. What if I had agreed to play some unfavorable role? I thought. Or be the best friend of this person, or the one who drives the car that hits his car, ending his life? I wondered. Suddenly, worry interrupted the joy that I normally experience here. I was able to quickly let go of my concerns, but I nevertheless kept looking at my skin to see if there was a blue glow indicating that it was my time to return to earth.

To further clarify my agreement with Glen, I went to talk to my teacher. He listened to my description of our meeting, then shook his head and said, "First and foremost, everyone makes agreements with individuals in their lives. As we walk through their life, particularly on earth, some of those agreements remain very strong, while others fade away because of choices that are made along the way. As people get ready to go back to a life on earth, they prepare, much like people would gather materials before building a house. I can't tell you what sort of agreement you have made with Glen, but I can tell you that as we become aware of how much we are connected to everything around us and how much we are prepared to live as an embodied spirit, many such agreements will manifest.

"When we have a sense of belonging to everything and feel the universal force through our bodies, we feel we have many friends among apparent strangers. So we don't meet a lot of individuals with whom we have *no* relationship. We feel we are all in relationships in one form or another, which leads to a more compassionate experience.

"Glen is going around gathering connections with individuals and opportunities for experiences because he has agreed to create a long life and wants it to be as rich and full as possible."

I then asked, "So we don't go back into an unconscious space where we do not understand that everything is spirit and matter?"

My teacher replied, "Correct—not that the lack of this awareness is a negative thing. But Glen fears losing deep connections he has had during many lives in the past. So he is gathering agreements with individuals who will remind him that he is spirit and matter, and that he is on the earth plane for a full life.

"Because Glen is going back soon and I made an agreement with him, does that mean I am going back soon?" I asked.

My teacher shook his head and said, "Glen is still gathering agreements. Yes, he is starting to show the blue color, which signals the transformation of cells that leads to the development of form. But Glen still has a little more time here, and so do you. So just relax and enjoy yourself."

For the first time, I had a sense that maybe when I come back to earth, I will be a teacher and will remember all the things that have been taught to me here. This thought carried me to a dream state for a while, and when I snapped back into a more conscious state my teacher was smiling at me—his biggest smile yet. I was somewhat unnerved by it, because showing emotions is something my teacher doesn't often do.

After I agreed with Glen to meet him in his next life on earth, I began imagining all kinds of different scenarios. But I soon realized it might be better to just be with this energy and to seek out just enough information to create a balance of knowledge, rather than too much information, which might overwhelm me. It is one thing to know that choices will be made in the future, but to ponder the infinite number of choices that aren't available can be unnerving.

I thanked my teacher and went back to my house, but I still couldn't help but wonder if my family and friends would be part of my next life, and whether I would recognize them—I hoped so.

Editor's note: Although many agreements between individuals concerning their lives on earth never manifest because of free-will choices made along the way, such agreements do become part of the fabric of our lives. Galen said it is not something to worry about or fear, and that moving with the flow of everything and remaining balanced makes it likely that such agreements will manifest. Galen said these conditions lead to a richer life experience. Heaven is the state of feeling connected to everything around us and all we experience through our lives. Even negative experiences have a purpose and meaning.

In a sense, lives are all sequenced in a way that allows individuals to have wonderful opportunities for growth and allows them to consciously see those opportunities as gifts. Understanding that all persons who come into our lives have a purpose for our development and understanding helps us better appreciate those people and our own growth process. From this perspective, even a total stranger saying hello at the grocery store may represent an agreement we once made, so appreciating those we meet as we experience our daily lives is important. Since the kaleidoscope of possibilities and probabilities of such agreements can overwhelm our minds, just focusing on whatever serves the highest good, without worrying much about the details, gives us the greatest freedom and the most chances for development.

CHAPTER 11

THE LAND OF DENIAL

After making my agreement with Glen, I thought a great deal about the process Glen was going through gathering experiences and agreements. I was curious about what kind of journey he was on, because I still did not know a lot about how much control individuals on the other side had concerning their futures and what role experiences and agreements played in that process. So one morning I decided I would take a long walk to see if I could connect to any realms new to me that might be important for my own future.

After going out my front door with Andy and Wyrme, I walked through a very beautiful area with blue skies, lush green grass, and majestic trees, all arranged in a wonderful way. Although the scenery kept changing as I proceeded, it retained the same quality of beauty. The more I thought about how lovely the scenery was, the more lovely it became, changes apparently reflecting my positive thoughts. After I had walked for what felt like one hundred miles, I decided to return home. Cresting a hill, I saw my house, despite having walked much farther *away* from my home than the distance required to return to it.

I knew this had happened because here one's thoughts can create a lot of one's environment, and when I had decided to go home, that intention made home appear more quickly. I went back inside and shook my head, thinking that certain experiences I have had did not seem to be only a reflection of my thoughts, and that others came from or went to places that I hadn't yet experienced, but I didn't know how to get there. I thought about this until I realized that thinking about it was part of the problem, because my mind did not have control over my environment and might be limiting my opportunities for new experiences, whereas if I didn't think of anything at all, perhaps I might get to some new realm.

The next day I again went on a long walk, accompanied by Andy and Wyrme, with renewed determination to see other places. This time I decided I would not think about it being a beautiful day or wonder where I was going, but remain neutral. This was not easy, because the environment looked very much like it had the day before—perhaps not quite with as much intensity of color or energy, but I concluded that this was probably because I was trying not to interact with it, so this would affect how it appeared. But despite remaining neutral, nothing changed substantially, which frustrated and disappointed me.

When I decided to go home, once again, just over the top of a hill was my house, precisely as the day before. This really confounded me, for it was like trying to think my way out of a box to something new. It made me claustrophobic to think that maybe there was no way to move out of the bubble of my realm. Then I had to remind myself that I had, in fact, already traveled through wormholes and portals and had also already had the experience of visiting other dimensional stations in my realm, such as when I visited my grandfather, Mr. Henderson. But my current desire was to gather experiences like Glen can from a different intention—not so much just curiosity or the wish to visit family members, but the will to learn and grow in the future. When you have the intention to visit a relative, you are drawn to them and a vibration with which you are already familiar. But now I was trying to visit parts of my realm without a clear connection to it. My dad once asked me about these other places, but I told him I had not explored them, because all I needed was the here and now of my dimensional station. But meeting Glen triggered my interest in these other places, because at some point something was going to shift for me here, and like Glen, I also might need to gather information and agreements in preparation for a return to earth. But I also realized now that even though I will be doing that sometime in the future, I can't control it simply through my will.

To focus less on expectations, the next day I decided not to insist to myself that I was going to take a journey that day, but instead I would only entertain ideas about how

I might get to other places that were part of my realm when the time was right.

So I set an intention in my mind that when I felt so inspired, I would travel to other parts of this dimension. And while I was not entirely certain this was the way to go about it, at least it felt like a clearer path than trying to force such travel. After this realization, I went out to have a regular day visiting some of my favorite hiking places, knowing my environment would respond to my desires.

One morning some days later, I woke up after having had a dream in which I had been traveling to places that looked and felt different. So I thought to myself, "Perhaps today is the day." I gathered my hiking gear and set out for a walk, along with Andy and Wyrme. Everything looked the same, but it felt like I was walking back on earth. The environment was neither engaging me nor ignoring me; it was simply just *there*, as it is on earth, where you are aware of it but don't interact with it, influencing its appearance. I covered a lot of distance in a very short time, which was also different from on previous attempts. I got excited about this, but I worried that by getting excited I would affect things again. Yet something inside reassured me that this was the right time for more exploration.

As I walked along, my skin seemed to be responding to something in the environment, something more powerful than just a change in temperature or wind direction. I then had a sense of pixilation taking place, as if I could see into the space between the pieces of the environment that made up this reality. I could make out people and trees, but such forms didn't have the usual coherence. Everything looked grainy and broken up, although Andy and Wyrme, who was on my shoulder, looked solid. I waited and just took in this new environment without moving forward, and then an adjustment took place that caused the grainy patterns to come together, making me feel like I could continue.

Now I saw a clearly defined sandy path through the grass and trees, as if someone had consciously created it. I walked about half a mile and saw that the path I had been walking on was leading back to the place where I had first started. It was then that I saw a force field that differentiated this new place from the one I had left.

I experimented by walking off the path a little to see if it would disappear when I wasn't walking on it, but it remained nevertheless, providing a clearly defined space that made me feel safe—safe because I didn't want to get trapped in a place that didn't resonate with me. I studied the people in this place, but they didn't look any different from the people in my realm.

I came upon a pleasant-looking, middle-aged woman sitting on a bench and throwing breadcrumbs to little birds congregated near her on the ground, a scene typical of any town park. I sat down next to her and said, "Hello, my name is Galen."

She looked up, startled, as she glanced with squinting eyes and answered, hesitantly, "Hello."

By now I realized that maybe she couldn't see me, so I asked her if she could see me and Andy.

She replied that she could barely make out a little of my form, almost as if I were transparent, but that she could see Andy's form better.

I further explained, "This is my first time in this realm. I decided to travel to see if there was anything other than what I have been experiencing since I've been here, and yours is the first area I came into."

"Oh…okay," she said politely, but in a way that indicated that whatever I just said put her off. I shared with her part of my story, just as I would in my home environment, including how I got here due to the train incident, the type of banter considered polite conversation in my realm. But the more I talked, the more uncomfortable she became.

"I am sorry, I don't mean to make you uncomfortable," I said.

"It's just that I really don't know what you are talking about," she replied. "Are you telling me you are dead?"

She said, clearly perturbed, "I…I don't know how to deal with that. Is your dog dead?"

I laughed and said, "I think he was once on earth and something happened to him that caused him to come to this dimension. But I really don't know for sure."

The longer we talked, the more I became visible to her, and eventually she could also make out Wyrme as he began to move, startling her.

"What is that thing around your neck?" she asked.

Then I explained how Wyrme and I had met, but that only upset her even more. Finally, she stood up and said, "You know, I really need to go. I have somewhere else to be."

"Before you go, can I ask you one thing? I realize this is upsetting you, and I don't mean to do that. But can you tell me if this is earth?"

"What is earth? What is that place you say you came from?" she replied.

Now perplexed myself, I looked at her closely, because I had some experience interacting with individuals who were not from earth, but everything about this woman told me that she had had a previous life on earth.

"Well, if this isn't earth, do you remember dying?" I asked.

Now she really looked frightened and confused, and she shook her head, saying, "I still don't know what you are talking about. What is dying? I think in asking such curious questions you are toying with me in some way, so I need to go. I think that is just what you are doing… asking curious questions and toying with me in some way, and I need to go."

She departed in such a hurry that she left her bag of crumbs. So, I sat on the bench and tossed the remaining crumbs to the birds, and wondered what had just happened. I then returned to the path but didn't make an attempt to talk, because they all seemed to be occupied, either talking to each other or focusing on doing something relaxing. When it got dark, I chose a spot under a tree to unpack my camping gear, have a little food, and get some rest.

The next morning when I awoke, I noticed people going about their business, but they were looking at me as if they could see me, which was interesting, because the day before no one was looking at me this way. I recognized the woman with whom I'd had the conversation standing among a small group gathered to check me out. "Well, this is either very good or not very good," I thought to myself.

As I tidied up, put everything in my backpack, and prepared to leave, the woman approached me and said, "Wait a minute. Are you Galen?"

"Yes, I am," I responded.

"I remember because you and your dog were in an upsetting dream I had last night," she explained.

"I don't know about it being a dream. I actually talked to you yesterday about where I came from while on that bench over there where you were feeding birds."

She looked confused and a little upset as she said, "That was what my dream was about. How could you know what my dream was about?" The group with her was nodding as she spoke, as if she had already told them all about her dream. She went on to explain some of the other things I told her the day before.

"Oh!" I said, realizing that she had convinced herself that she had had a precognitive dream about me rather than actually meeting me. It occurred to me that whatever this woman was doing, she clearly was part of the dimension I was in, but from a realm that allowed for disconnection from the surrounding energy, thus not permitting people to gain a true sense of where they were or what they were doing and learning. Even I had some difficulty figuring things out here.

I now realized that everyone here had some level of disconnection from what was actually happening to them, and much less awareness than in my realm. Everyone was happy—no one looked lost or depressed or clueless—but they had no idea about energy, death, or even what they had experienced the day before. Apparently, anything beyond what was happening in the present, that was predictable, and didn't require any deep thought frightened the people in this place, so for them safety trumped reality. It was as if they were stuck in a place of denial.

"I am getting ready to go now and follow this path," I said, gesturing in the path's direction.

"Okay," they said, making expressions that indicated they could not see the path. I waved goodbye, and after walking a while, I sat down and wrote about everything I had experienced, thinking I would ask my teacher about it because I did not understand what was going on here.

I walked again until the sun started to set and then made preparations to sleep next to the path.

Editor's note: The experiences of the people in the realm Galen visited would certainly be considered limited by the standards of Galen's dimensional station, where everything is possible and anything can happen. I asked Galen about the common thread among all who inhabited this Land of Denial, as I call it, and was told it was a deep fear of change to the point where stability was their fortress. But that doesn't mean that people who are afraid of change will end up in this realm. Apparently, it is not a punishment to be in it, but it evidently is a place needed for people's fear to be released. Galen likely was one of many visitors who passed through the realm, changing things in it because without such catalysts to help things shift, no one in the realm would ever be able to leave.

Since eventually the fear such people have of change is released, and the fear of change does not bring punishment on the other side, the Land of Denial ultimately seems like a compassionate realm. Galen has said that the many levels he has visited do not involve punishment, but rather learning and alignment with universal laws. Further, the fabric of people's natures and experiences are what these realms are made of. So they are not separate from us but places we create, along with others who share similar patterns or vibrations.

I did have a question about whether the inhabitants of the Land of Denial had silver cups. After all, if they were in denial about their transition, wouldn't they be in denial about having silver cups? Indeed, there were no silver cups to be seen. Now, a cup is an archetype, which for Galen represented a vessel of purity. However, at Galen's dimensional station the cup does not need to be a cup, but it needs to be something so the individual has awareness that they are carrying this with them for a while.

The Land of Denial is inhabited by those whose personalities are not only strong, but do not want change. The ego is in charge, but there are not many who can hold denial to such a degree that they deny their own transition. Still, there are enough. However, one can only hold that position for so long, and it will shift and change so that truth eventually forces its way into their reality. But denial is a very powerful emotion. In the case of the inhabitants of the Land of Denial, they carried the energy of the cup, but as they would not focus on it, the cup did not manifest as an object they could see.

CHAPTER 12

REALM OF THE WATER PEOPLE

I woke up and put together my things in preparation to go further down the path, still thinking about how strange it was that individuals in the realm I had just visited seemed to be so disconnected from the energy of the realm.

I could clearly see the path up ahead as it wound through a thick grove of some of the tallest trees I had ever seen, like redwoods but not standing together so densely that the sun didn't shine through to the forest floor. The scene had an amazing energy. Yet everything looked familiar—not so much the sense that I had created it, but as if I were remembering it from somewhere, though not from my earth life.

As I walked along, I saw sometimes a glint of light reflecting off tree trunks, and the further I walked, the more tree trunks showed this lovely sparkle. Stepping off the path to investigate, I saw that in the vertical grooves of bark on the trunks where one might expect to find moss, there were beautiful, perfectly formed little crystals growing—the source of the reflections I had been seeing. I was astonished at how two elements that normally would not have been connected to each other on earth—crystals and trees—were growing together here, with the crystals apparently enhancing the energy of the trees.

Though the phenomenon was counter to my expectation of things, I enjoyed it immensely. And even though Andy seemed fine, the energy appeared to have put Wyrme in a trancelike state; the patterns in its fur changed quickly, almost as if it were transmitting these patterns as signals to the trees. I worried about the energy being overwhelming for Wyrme, because it felt forceful. But I couldn't ask Wyrme to compact itself down, so I just walked with great caution, because I had no idea what would happen to Wyrme if, in its present state, it fell off my shoulders to the ground.

As I came close to the end of this forest, after about another three or four miles, I could hear the sound of water, as if there were an ocean just ahead. I kept up a steady pace, hoping when I was clear of the trees Wyrme would return to its former self, and Andy quickened his pace, moving toward the opening up ahead.

Finally I walked out of the forest, but there was no ocean or other body of water. Instead, there was a green meadow with many flowers. I moved to the middle of the meadow, where I couldn't see anything except for the path. I shrugged my shoulders, trying to understand why I had heard the sound of water. Fortunately, Wyrme was now behaving normally again, purring loudly as if what it had just experienced had made it happy, rather than been threatening. I felt a little revved up, as if I had just taken some super vitamins.

I continued walking again. I went quite a distance, but the water sound I had heard before remained omnipresent. Finally, I saw a small group of people moving together in the field, slightly bent over in the waist-high grass, apparently doing something methodically, such as harvesting or picking something up. I hurried ahead, but because of the grass, I could not see them clearly until I was right upon them.

Then I was shocked when I saw that every one of these individuals was encased in a bubble of water that was clear and clean with only the slightest hint of blue, and although a water current was moving around their bodies, they were not drowning.

I realized that it must have been from these people that I was hearing what sounded like the ocean. Standing directly in front of them, the sound was quite loud. I said, "Hello," and they returned the greeting. Then I gave them my name and told them I was following the path.

"Oh, okay," they all said in unison, but it was clear they didn't see the path, which was apparently only visible to me. Perhaps they thought I meant "path" in a different way. No one seemed to notice that I was not encased in a bubble of water or showed that they found my dry state curious. Nor did they ask what I was doing here or where I was going, unlike the people the day before who had asked many questions.

I wanted to know where their homes were, because these people were just out in the middle of a field. So I asked, "Where do you live?"

"Just over in that direction is our village," they all replied.

"Are there more of you?" I asked.

"Oh yes, there are many more," said the man closest to me, who was helpful but didn't offer his name. Since they seemed friendly, I continued chatting with him as the group moved forward in the field, noticing that these individuals were creating a very peaceful atmosphere, as if they were of one mind. I also noticed that whenever the man moved in any way, such as turning and pointing to the village, everyone else mimicked his movements. Further, the sounds of water were almost in sync with the sounds of the wind sweeping through the grass. In fact, everything seemed to be coordinated and in harmony.

Since my path was leading in the direction where the man had pointed, I proceeded to a place where the field stopped, and although I saw several beautifully manicured spaces and flower gardens, as well as areas with chairs, lamps, and rugs, I didn't see any structures. Several of these "rooms" without structures around them were populated with people in groups of between five and seven, all engaged industriously in exactly the same activities. Because they acted as a group, I figured out pretty quickly that I should engage with them as a group rather than individually, as it was probably considered rude to make individual conversation.

Finding the lack of structures curious, and intrigued with their surroundings, I went up to one group and explained the kind of journey I was on and that I had never encountered anyone encased in a bubble of water. I had seen people who had been separated, such as people who had committed suicides, in enclosed windows, but I had never seen people in water. The people in the group looked at each other perplexed, which caused the water surrounding them to shimmer, as if circulating faster around their bodies, rather than just flowing with their movements.

"Obviously you are not from our village, but we are not sure what you mean by water around us," they said.

I did my best to explain, even drawing an illustration of what I was seeing in the dirt. But they didn't see themselves enclosed in bubbles of water; they just saw themselves as being the same, which was probably why they all acted alike, as if they were part of a school of fish.

How could they not notice that they were enclosed in bubbles of water? I wondered. But maybe if they couldn't see water around themselves, they also couldn't see the water around anyone else either. Emotionally, they were not separate from each other, as they were friendly and engaging people who moved in groups, completely in sync with whatever was in their vicinity. Yet they were separate from their environment. I wondered whether people from other realms coming into mine would also see me differently than I see myself.

I stayed with these people for a couple of days, because it was fascinating to watch how everyone worked together, and I enjoyed my connection to them. I speculated that they had no need for shelter, because in their emotional space the constant sound of water provided a feeling of having shelter. As time passed, I became used to the sound, and it eventually moved to the background, just as if I were at the seashore and tuned out the constant crashing of waves on the beach. And even though they did not have answers for everything in this realm, I did learn a lot from my observations.

Editor's note: Galen surmised that the path, surrounded by redwoods in whose bark crystals grew, separated two realms. The energy field in the trees seemed to make it easier for Galen to adapt to the new realm, whereas he had had difficulty adapting to the previous realm he had visited. Wyrme reacted to this energy in a different way, by processing this shift while still remaining connected to Galen.

When I asked Galen if the people he had encountered in this realm were not humans but were pods of cetaceans that Galen saw as humans, Galen told me that later he had learned that many of these individuals had led very empathic earth lives in which they were able to constantly feel the energy around them, and while some could manage this well, the lives of others had been shattered by it, although not their spirits or souls. They then had chosen to connect to a very primal source of energy and information—water.

Every one of them was empathic to the point where they had connected to a primal core of themselves during their earth lives and now worked with this aspect of their emotional nature. They also seemingly had an empathic connection to cetaceans, but they had not been cetaceans themselves. And the group activity they were engaging in when Galen first saw them in the field was a way of aligning their energy fields.

CHAPTER 13

REALM OF LOVE

As I walked away from the realm of people who were encased in bubbles of water, I felt a longing to be back in their world. On one level I felt isolated with them, because I was not having the same experience as they were, but on another level, associating with a group of people living without walled structures was comforting and made me yearn for a deeper sense of belonging. As I walked along, I realized this was something I had struggled with inwardly on earth—constantly trying to belong but instead having a sense of otherness, making me wonder where my rightful place, or authentic self, was. Walking farther, with Andy pacing along by my side and Wyrme on my shoulders humming, I was soon back in the quiet forest with the clearly visible path.

I paused for a moment to experience the muted light filtering through the trees. In that moment, I noticed moving circles of muted colors among the trees—like one sees when dizzy. But it wasn't due to my vision, because I held my hand out in front of my eyes and saw no visual disturbances.

This excited me, as I realized I was probably getting close to another new realm, because each time I moved into a different realm there was some sort of energetic boundary I had to cross, and this is what the circles of color were. The farther I walked, the more the circles of color danced around when I focused on something in the distance. It made me a little dizzy but became lighter and brighter in a certain color range—mostly oranges and greens. Now there were borders around the spots, as if they were two-dimensional illustrations. And the tree trunks also changed from having an organic appearance to having the appearance of geometric designs. Even on the path ahead of me, everything started to have green and orange borders. I changed my assumption that I had passed the boundary from one realm to another and now believed I had only just begun the transition. Gradually, more geometric shapes of all varieties were replacing the organic ones, and the colors were becoming increasingly brighter.

The way my feet felt when placed on the ground had also changed, now feeling as if they were landing slightly above the surface of the path, so it took a moment or two to become sure-footed. And everything looked like it was floating slightly above its environment, so nothing was anchored or had a foundation.

Andy's appearance was now also made of geometric shapes—tiny squares, circles, and triangles. I could sense by Andy's eyes that he was having the same experience, seeing me as composed of geometric shapes, and his response was to bark playfully like a puppy and run off the path into the grass, which now appeared as stacks of elongated triangles that would break into other geometric patterns as he ran through them. Everything was alive with light, shapes, and colors, as if dancing. However, my body and Wyrme had not changed, although my clothing was composed of geometric shapes. I felt like doing a little experiment, so I gently poked at Wyrme, hoping it would compact down into a ball. I could feel vibration coming at me from Wyrme, but not the usual pleasant vibration, and I knew it was reluctant to comply. Finally, Wyrme shrank down into a ball, so I put it in my shirt pocket, and then my hands also transformed into geometric shapes to match everything else in this environment. Looking at my hands was like looking at very intricate stained glass. If I looked at them from a distance, they only had five rectangles on a square, but as I moved the hands closer, I could see finer and finer detail in the geometric shapes.

Then I pulled Wyrme out of my pocket, held it in my palm, and gently blew on it, the signal to expand again. The minute I was in contact with Wyrme's normal tubular shape, my body no longer had geometric shapes. This made me believe Wyrme was changing the shape everything else had, and given that Wyrme's properties are a mystery, I didn't know if I would ever understand the reason behind it.

I continued on the path and occasionally noticed forms that looked like animals or birds, and then I came across what I thought were people moving through the grass.

Andy ran up to one of them, wagging his geometric tail. I saw a being reach down and pet Andy the same way I would greet a dog. Andy barked joyously and almost danced on his hind legs, as if he knew these people. As I walked toward one of the figures, I saw that these beings were not flesh-covered forms like humans, but like entities of light, with more light coming from them than anything else in the surroundings.

"Hello, I am Galen, traveling through this lovely world. Do you live here?" I asked.

At this point I could sense vibrations coming toward me, and in perhaps the purest tone I had ever heard, the being responded, "No, we don't live here, but we visit often. It is quite lovely, isn't it?"

"It is amazing," I agreed. "I could not have even imagined such a place. The closest thing I have ever seen before is stained-glass computer-generated art."

This being waved over two other figures, and I could hear the first being say, "Ah, yes, that would be a good comparison."

The other two beings, who now approached, were composed of the same bright white tones. I greeted them as well, then said, "You say you come here often to visit, and I understand why. But during this journey I am also trying to find out some information, as I want to understand my experiences better." I even explained that I was sharing this information with my father, who would be listening to this conversation eventually.

Then I asked, "Did you come from earth?"

"No, we have a different connection to the earth plane," one being said.

"I can't really make out your form. Are you human?" I asked.

"No, we are not human," said another.

With growing curiosity, I then asked, "Are you from another planet?" I mentioned I had met a few friends from different planets back in the school in my realm.

"No, we are not from a different planet," said another.

Now I got concerned, as I recalled encountering beings from parallel universes, but Andy was so joyful in the presence of these individuals that I dismissed my concern. "Okay, are you angels?" I asked.

"No, we are not angels," one answered.

"What are you?" I finally asked.

"We are part of spirit; we are part of light—you would likely know us as guides and inner voices. We are connected to 'allness.'"

"If you are just part of spirit and light, why do you have forms?" I asked. They then told me that in their normal routines they don't have bodies, which is why they love coming to this realm, where they have some form and experience things in a different way.

"We come when others travel through this realm so we can help them absorb and understand their experiences. For instance, when you entered this realm, you did not know at first how to appreciate your sensual experiences of beauty and form," they explained.

"Are you my guides? Have you known me before?" I asked.

"We have always known you, Galen. We have traveled with you many, many times, and we are always invisible to you."

I had no idea how to respond to that. It was a powerful experience to actually meet personified as form inner guides who have provided love and guidance in the past. I now understood why Andy was so joyful when we first encountered these beings or forms of energy.

I remained silent for a moment, watching the grass wave, listening to a light tinkling sound, and absorbing the beauty around me, including the three beings in front of me. Then I began to cry—not because of sadness or a sense of loss, but because I was experiencing the purest connectedness that I had ever felt. That moment changed me. All the other experiences I have had in this dimension, though not in linear time, have had a sequence, allowing me to adjust emotionally and psychologically as I went along. But here the totality of everything just rushed through me, and when it did, I heard the purest singing, like one might imagine angels to sound like. However, it was not coming from these beings of light. Surprisingly, it was coming from Wyrme. Wyrme was completely extended out, vibrating in an incredible way, and making this beautiful sound. Andy, myself, and the three beings listened intently as this song came out of Wyrme. When Wyrme became silent again, the beings bowed to Andy and Wyrme, petting it before they blended into all the geometric forms of the energy field enveloping us, while I felt purified inside and out.

Soon Wyrme went back to purring on my shoulders, and Andy came over to my side like he was ready to go. So I walked away from one of the most beautiful places I had ever been. I feel, at some level, that this realm was where all the love comes from, and is then shared with all the worlds. It really was like heaven, or what I imagine heaven might be, and I knew I would carry this energy with me for the rest of my time. As I continued walking on the path, it was difficult to leave that beautiful realm, but I realized I could always come back and be a part of this geometric realm. I knew that part of me is there and has always been there.

Editor's note: The realm Galen describes, with its environment like a cubist painting, may have been what is called the causal plane, recognizable to me because I have been there, although not as completely as Galen.

Galen clarified that the beings he encountered there, although guides, never said they were only his guides. Galen's experience with the light beings was so pure and profound that it left an impression beyond what the mind can comprehend. And even Wyrme was so affected by their energy that it produced the purest sound Galen had ever heard this creature make, rivaling the sound of angels singing. Encountering these beings no doubt brought Galen closer to a sense of spirit and the divine connecting everything in the universe. The joy Galen felt in the presence of the beings was the closest he has ever come to experiencing pure love. These beings who chose to communicate with Galen could, perhaps, be seen as personifications of the entity that channels love to the entire universe.

The three beings do not belong to any one dimension or form; they belong to all and are connected to everyone. Galen said that meeting them was perhaps the purest expression of Source that he had ever experienced, and while they were not connected to one particular dimension, his presence in this particular realm activated their energy and caused them to manifest. So Galen had a sense that it really wasn't about him. While they acknowledged they knew him, Source (light, color, and sound) travels everywhere. And since when light, color, and sound come together they manifest geometric form, so it is not surprising to find that Source could express itself that way in the realm Galen visited.

Galen said as he actually became the experience, experiencing a direct link from Source to soul, and he had a sense of feeling complete, and that if others would only risk such a journey, they would likely come across that level of beauty in their own lives.

Galen also told me that when he cried, he was able to let go of everything and felt that, for the first time, he'd stepped into a pure dimension, not one conceived to bring forth certain responses. His experience was so profound he will carry it with him always.

CHAPTER 14

THE CITY OF "LIKE HINDSIGHT"

The path was now leading me into an open range of grass that gradually turned from green to straw-colored, looking much like a flat prairie. The earth underneath the drying grass was pale, as if it didn't contain a lot of nutrients or moisture. I felt some hesitation, and it seemed Andy had some as well, for he walked so close to my legs that I almost tripped over him, while Wyrme seemed indifferent. I thought about how different this new landscape was, even though it was somehow familiar. There was something unwelcoming about its expansiveness and dryness, giving me a feeling of vulnerability, as if I could get lost here, even though the path was clearly demarcated and I could see it ahead of me for what seemed miles. The farther I walked, the less inviting the area became, with the grass becoming increasingly sparse and the soil a chalky white. I thought about the story *The Little Prince*, in which the prince walks around the world, as well as other stories of adventure, trying to entertain and energize myself, because if I just tuned into the landscape, I felt drained.

Andy looked up at me and half wagged his tail, but his ears drooped, so I felt concerned. Although I had seen Andy act protectively in the past, I had never seen him act this way, and I wondered if it reflected dejection or danger. Clearly, he was very different here from the happy dog I had witnessed in the realm I had just left. Usually I would see somebody in each realm I was in, but here there was no one. I stopped and listened, but all I could hear was the wind. This seemed strange, because I had thought every realm functioned purposefully to provide experience for individuals whose beliefs brought them there. Then I wondered if this realm was a place whose purpose was to catalyze reflection.

Finally, the grass started to appear increasingly greener, and soon I saw trees and shrubs in the distance, providing a feeling of great relief. Andy raced ahead of me to the trees marking the perimeter of this realm, and then stopped in their shade to wait for me, so eager was he to get out of this space. As I reached the trees where Andy waited, he was looking back toward the place where we had just been walking, so I turned around to look myself, and saw everywhere thousands of residential structures of all shapes and sizes, all the same color of the bleached dirt, along with streetlights. I was astonished by the sudden appearance of what seemed like a busy city.

I thought that perhaps I should go back and take another look, thinking maybe this was a place you could only see by looking backward. So, I stepped back onto the path, but very quickly Andy tugged me back. I didn't feel any danger, but Andy was rarely so insistent, so I paid attention to his instinct and backed up into the trees. In the split second before Andy pulled me back, when both my feet were on the path, the city shimmered as if it were a mirage. But as soon as I was back in the shade of the trees, the city again appeared solid. This made me want to investigate even more, so I stepped back on the path and told Andy, "Hold on, I am not going back but just checking something." Once again, the city started to shimmer like a mirage and begin to fade but then appeared solid again as I stepped back into the trees. I decided to sit down under a tree and just watch the city for a while to see what would happen to its appearance.

I observed that the inhabitants of the city were very busy. I watched some of the structures being constructed and then being taken down, as if the builders had changed their minds. There were people walking in the streets, but they didn't interact with each other beyond nodding their heads to acknowledge each other. I wondered why I hadn't been able to see the city while I had been walking through it.

Finally, at Andy's urging, I continued on the path away from the city and into another forested area. Off to the side of the forest entrance, hanging on a tree, was a brochure box, exactly like something at a trailhead in a national park on earth. I picked up one of the brochures, which showed pictures of the city, but there wasn't anything printed in it that provided answers about why I hadn't been able to see this city when I was standing in the middle of it.

I stuffed the brochure back in the box, because I didn't feel the need to take it with me, but as I walked away, I heard a voice ask, "Aren't you going to take that with you?"

I turned around to see a short man standing there—not a troll or an elf but an ordinary human—dressed like a park ranger. I shook my head thinking this was a little crazy that right next to the brochure box would be a park ranger ready to answer questions.

"I didn't understand what the brochure said, and I didn't feel a need to take it with me because I am not returning," I explained to the ranger.

"You are not going to come back?" he asked, seemingly perplexed.

"No, I am not going to go back. And what are you doing here?" I asked.

"This is my home, my job—to help visiting individuals understand what they just passed through," he replied.

I didn't completely trust that this man was real, as he was like a fictional character in books I had read and because everything else seemed to be an illusion, so I gently poked him to see if he was really there.

"Oh, I get that often," the park ranger said, laughing at my gesture.

"I am sorry, I wasn't sure if you were real," I said, embarrassed.

"I am real," the park ranger replied.

"Then can you tell me why I didn't see the city when I was walking through it but only when I looked back at it? And why would my dog pull me back when I wanted to go back and investigate the city?"

"Going through it you had no idea what you were doing, seeing, or what to expect, but when you turned around, you saw everything—like when one can see things in hindsight. Your dog pulled you back because he had great wisdom, knowing that often it is not wise to go back over things that you have just been through, that people can get stuck in such spaces. In short, this city is the place where it is possible to see things in hindsight, and where one realizes one can't go back to the past—like your dog tried to help you understand," the park ranger explained.

"Are you telling me this realm is called Hindsight?"

"No," he said, "this realm is called 'Like Hindsight.'"

"Are the people living and working there trapped somehow? Did they try to live in the past?" I asked, feeling like I had been caught in some realm in *Alice in Wonderland*.

"No one is really stuck there, but some people refuse to leave. However, eventually they discover that they can't live in this place—when they see the same materials being repeatedly used to build with in the same spaces and are able to leave as they recognize patterns of activity."

This gradually made sense to me, as I had been becoming more aware of the dangers of dwelling in the past through lessons in my realm. Now, apparently, I had seen a visual representation of this principle.

I said, "Thank you very much. I am on a journey, and I have a sense I need to be heading back home."

Nodding, the park ranger added, "Have a good journey, Galen, but be sure and take a brochure with you."

"Why would I need it?" I asked, perplexed.

"Because sometimes having hindsight can help you be very creative and move forward faster. You have a lot of changes ahead of you. You have experienced hindsight before, but what's up ahead of you is very new and unique, and you are going to need a little hindsight when you move forward," he explained.

I took a brochure just in case I would need it, as the park ranger had seemed knowledgeable. Then I thanked him again and walked down the path through the beautiful woods with Andy and Wyrme.

Editor's note: When I asked Galen if there was any additional explanation of why he did not see the city of "Like Hindsight" and was told that it was because he was forward-thinking and trying to get to the other side of this space in a hurry, in part perhaps because of the fear of getting stuck in that energy field, he was projecting a lot of energy toward the future, and so didn't have hindsight. This is true of anyone who focuses too intently on what is ahead—they don't see in hindsight.

Once in the safety of the trees Galen could look back and see the city of "Like Hindsight," but it didn't serve him to go back because the experience had gone by.

People can certainly get stuck living in the past. The city of "Like Hindsight" was well populated, so many who have crossed over must live in the past, although the park ranger provided the hopeful perspective that these people eventually do move on to new experiences.

CHAPTER 15

THE GOLDEN REVOLVING DOOR

As I moved forward, the forest around me became thicker, and I had to be careful of where I was placing my feet, because there were pieces of branches on the path, as if someone had sprinkled wood chips on the forest floor so I could clearly see it. There were even signs pointing to various trails one could take with funny names like "Angel Trail" and "Diamond Trail." I was delighted that the "park theme" was being carried through here, following my experience with the diminutive park ranger.

I took my time walking so I could enjoy the scenery, with light filtering through the thick canopy of trees and birds flitting around. After a while there were no more signs or wood chips on the path, and up ahead I could see it growing ever lighter.

Then the path started to incline, and I could also see that I had a very large hill to climb. But unlike an earth trail, the path here was without scattered rocks or debris. As I continued, the hill became steeper and steeper and now required a lot of effort. A couple of times I had to reach out and grab some of the brush next to the path to pull myself up. I was using all my strength to keep going and began to worry that I wasn't going to make it to the top.

Just as I thought I was going to have to crawl the rest of the way, I could see the top ahead. But I thought Andy couldn't make it. So when I made it to the crest, I grabbed him behind the neck with my right arm and put my left behind his right leg and lifted him up. We both took a well-needed rest on the plateau where we now were.

As Andy and I sat facing the direction from which we had come, I could feel Wyrme stretching out on my shoulders, humming excitedly. It prompted me to spin around and look up ahead at the path, where there was a gentle downgrade through a green meadow, in the middle of which was an intense white light.

Although Andy was pretty tired after the climb up the hill, we started walking together down the slope toward the light. The grass, which was very soft with new feathery seed heads forming, was being swept around very gently by the wind.

Now I felt pulsing coming from the light source, similar to the one Wyrme creates. As I walked closer, the pulsing grew stronger, which made me somewhat nervous. Then I put my hand in front of my eyes and parted my fingers ever so slightly to diffract the light, allowing me to make out a shape in the center of the bright light of a seven-sided, golden-yellow building, with soft pink, blue, and purple undertones. The colors rotated, so a particular side was never the same color. The light was coming through the building's golden doorway, which rotated as well. When the doorway wasn't directly in front of me, I was able to get a better view of the building, and I noticed it was floating off the ground.

I first wondered whether the light might be coming from a spaceship of some kind, because of the almost industrial hum it emitted, as if it might have an engine. When I saw that my path went directly to this building, I panicked a little, as I wasn't sure that I actually wanted to walk into it. But Andy was sitting calmly next to me, looking at it, which was important, because I read the reactions of my companions as clues about my safety. Wyrme continued to be excited, straining toward it, trying to match the building's rhythmic pulsing with its own, and Wyrme's body began to take on the same colors the building displayed.

I walked around the building before I ventured where the path was leading me, but as I did so the grass became uninviting, with the seeds catching to my clothes. When the golden door rotated in front of me, not only was there a path through it, but the pulsing I had been feeling was drawing me in. Finally I stepped toward the golden door and found myself on the other side in an instant, but much farther down the path than I should have been based on the number of steps I had taken. The building was now only a small spot on the horizon, and it was almost as if time or space had shifted. I continued walking forward, but Andy looked hesitant, and I could not find Wyrme anywhere.

Panicking, I ran back to the building, scanning the path as I ran, but I saw no trace of Wyrme. As I reached the building and the golden doorway appeared in front of me, I could see through to the other side, but the landscape showing was not where I had just been. I did not know what to do, but when the door swung back around, Andy leaped through it, and I reached forward in time to catch his tail and go through the passage.

Once again, we were on a path. But far down it, the building was back in the distance, and there was still no sign of Wyrme. The trees around me were not the same; instead of pines there were shimmering golden aspens, like those I used to see in the mountains above Santa Fe in early October. On seeing this new vista, I was even more frightened than I had been. Here the air felt cooler, and it was a different season—conditions I felt I had not chosen. I turned to Andy and said, "We have to find Wyrme. This isn't the path we were on before."

Andy turned his head toward me and barked, acknowledging that he understood completely what I had said to him. We walked back to the building to wait for the golden door to appear in front of us, and we leaped in again, only to find ourselves in a new area on a path that ended abruptly at an ocean. I looked back to see the golden building off in the distance and became fearful again, more for myself than for Wyrme, because I had encountered something that kept putting me in unfamiliar places that didn't feel like part of my journey. Even though I never knew what to expect in each of the realms through which I had walked up until now, they had felt somewhat familiar and seemed to pertain to my journey.

But my new environment felt alien and separate from my journey. Furthermore, I had lost my valuable companion, Wyrme, making me feel uncomfortable and unsafe. In the past, even in the most intense moments, I always had Wyrme with me to comfort and reassure me. Now I wondered if my constant connection to Wyrme had given me the courage to do what I had been doing, because Wyrme had always anchored me in some way. Anxious and ashamed at being afraid, I joked with myself, "What are you afraid of? Do you think you might die?"

After reflecting on my situation and summoning my courage, I formulated a plan to keep going back and forth until I found the place I had originally come from before I went through the golden door. But I also decided that if I had to go ahead without Wyrme, I would do so, realizing that since Wyrme had found his way to me before, it could do it again. But each time Andy and I leaped through the door we ended up in a very different environment, including a snowy landscape that felt like Antarctica, where it was too cold for Andy and me to remain long.

As I kept repeatedly going through the door, worried about reconnecting with Wyrme and finding very different environments that didn't feel right, finally something told me not to leap through the door anymore but to walk through it slowly, to perhaps gain greater insight into which direction to go. So Andy and I walked slowly toward the golden door, and instantly it stopped being a revolving door.

Once we walked into the building, I could see everything in every direction, and I knew I could choose which direction to go rather than chance taking me in various directions. I could not only see what option the golden door offered, but I could see where each side of the building led, as if the wall of each colored side were transparent. The strong energy inside the building now felt welcoming, because it was like having warm sunlight on my face, a kind of energy I had not experienced since the first moments after I passed and had arrived on the other side.

At that time, I had felt this kind of loving energy during conversations with my teacher when I was making the initial choice to cross over to the other side. Now, standing in the center of the building, I closed my eyes as I thanked the welcoming energy that gave me a sense of feeling loved, connected, and understood—a sense of Source. As I reached over to stroke Andy's head, I could feel him lean into me with deep appreciation. Then, unconsciously, I reached up to my shoulder, and there was Wyrme, sitting there as usual. I was overjoyed and felt deep gratitude for again being with both my companions in this place of loving energy. At this point it occurred to me that perhaps one purpose of the frightening experience of being lost and isolated had been to bring me to a state where I would take the time to feel greater gratitude for the opportunities I had had for experiencing positive energy during my journey.

Then as I watched the door again revolve, this time from inside, I soon saw the initial environment with the soft, feathery grass and the path. Very slowly, Wyrme,

Andy, and I stepped through the door and back onto the path. And when I turned around to look at the building, it was right there next to me. Because the light wasn't overwhelming any longer, I could now see its beautiful form and color, turning like a revolving jewel box, pausing slightly as each colorful side came into view. It now gave me the sense that it was not frightening, as I better understood its rhythm, timing, and function.

Feeling that I had learned a lesson and thus concluded a part of my journey, I decided to head home.

Editor's note: Galen felt that the golden building was a crossroads where he had to calmly and consciously decide his next step. He said that the building felt like a temple, and by reaching it and understanding the lesson it offered, he had achieved what he had set out to do on this particular journey.

Galen told me further that because of its grandeur and the subtle movement, the building was "like the timepiece of the universe."

The day before Galen told me about these experiences, I felt his presence with me so strongly that I would not have been shocked to have seen him standing in front of me. When I had the sensation that he was there, I was emotionally transported to a scene in *The Subtle Knife*, the second novel in the book *His Dark Materials* series (*The Golden Compass*), written by English novelist Philip Pullman. It was as if I was in the story, going through portals created by using the subtle knife, traveling to alternate realities and experiencing being in a place where I felt I don't belong and with which I have no connection.

This allowed me to better appreciate how Galen felt when he found himself in a strange realm without Wyrme, the creature that had always been Galen's bridge to energies found in them.

In relating these experiences to me, it seemed to me that Galen was preparing me emotionally to understand what it felt like in this otherworld of the golden building. Galen stated that it wasn't a wormhole, saying, "I have been in a wormhole, and I know what that feels like. But this came from a very intentional space, from Source." When I asked about the cause of Wyrme's disappearance, Galen told me that later he realized that in reality Wyrme had been in the center of this building the whole time and was thus never really lost. It wasn't until Galen overcame his fear and stood inside the building, instead of leaping through its door, that he reconnected with Wyrme. He also reminded me that Wyrme has a bit of an addiction to certain energy fields, especially one that felt like home, and it didn't need someone to help it connect or balance itself. Eventually, Galen had mastered whatever body-mind-spirit state was necessary to use the building as a tool.

CHAPTER 16

THE STONE CLACKERS

I was excited at the thought of going home and eager to speak with my teacher again. When I had started on my journey, I had been a bit apprehensive about the unknown, but now I had a sense of satisfaction and peacefulness, like something had been answered for me. Although all my experiences had contributed in some way to my new confidence and sense of accomplishment, it was pretty clear to me that on exiting the golden door I had gained the most significant insights.

I felt so refreshingly carefree that I sang and danced a little, while Andy pranced around and Wyrme hummed. Soon I realized I had walked the distance I usually walked before coming to a boundary between realms. Eventually, I was delighted to see ahead some beautiful mountains, blue sky, the sunshine, and trees that looked familiar, like something that would manifest when I set out intentionally to create a landscape.

I stopped for a moment when I heard in the distance a loud clacking sound, as if someone was constructing something with a hammer. Sometimes I heard just one such sound, but other times a multitude of clacks repeated three times. The clacking would reach a crescendo, then change to random clacking, then stop completely before resuming again. In between intervals of clacking, I would strain to hear the sounds again, not only to figure out what they were but because I somehow felt connected to their rhythm.

I was curious about the sounds because they seemed to be coming from the mountains I thought I had created, and when I create something like a landscape, usually no one else, other than Andy and Wyrme, intervenes.

Fifteen minutes later, after hearing the sounds again, I stopped and listened very carefully to the number of clacks and the timing of them until I was sure of the pattern.

Now the path was curving away from the mountains, even though the sounds were still growing louder. Soon I walked into a field where a man was sitting on a rock, looking like a wizard, not unlike the rock I liked to sit on back home. He was dressed in robes, had long gray hair and a long gray beard, and held two large, smooth river stones, one in each hand. He stood up and started banging the stones together in the same rhythm of clacks that I had been hearing.

Knowing the rhythm I had heard, I surmised his clacking would be followed by that of others. I looked around, but I couldn't see anyone else in this grassy field. But a moment later, just before the second clacking sound was due, according to the timing and rhythm I had heard before, there appeared another man who looked almost exactly like the first, down to the long gray hair and beard. He joined in, and soon the two men were joined by a third, a fourth, and a fifth, all appearing at the right time to maintain the rhythm.

When the time for random clacking came, they didn't stop making sounds, but kept the stones in contact, grinding them in a circular pattern to create a certain tone for several minutes. As each man did this, a bubble came up around him and he floated around in this field as if in a hot-air balloon. The faster they rubbed the stones, the more they would move around. Also, when the part of the cycle with the bubbles began, the whole area was encircled by a group of smaller bubbles that seemed to just float up from the ground. Then they slowed down the grinding, and their bubbles landed on the ground, popped, and the men disappeared. Further, Andy's energy field changed, as if someone was projecting faces and patterns onto his body, until the men vanished and Andy appeared again without any such patterns, as if he was reflecting what was happening to the men. I stood there with my mouth open in amazement, having no idea what I was witnessing.

Then I waited, because if my calculation about the cycle was correct, the men would reappear. And they did. First, just one appeared and started the rhythm, and then at intervals the others showed up again, repeating the same sounds and actions. I tried to engage with them, but they would not even acknowledge me. I even walked up to one of the men and touched him to see if he was solid, which momentarily disrupted his rhythm, but still the men didn't react to me. Baffled, I wondered if these men were projections, like the projected images I saw on Andy.

The men seemed very different from all the other beings I had met, yet at the same time the scene had great appeal and beauty, and the tone and rhythm were quite alluring. I wondered if these men were performing a purification ritual, like the shimmering energy band that had passed through my realm.

Ultimately, I had to move on from this beautiful mystery between cycles to avoid walking into any bubbles blocking my way, just in case they were passages to other realms like the golden door. This mystery just added to my desire to return home, so I could ask my teacher what I had been watching in this realm.

As the sound of the stone clappers started to fade away, I was reviewing everything I had gone through on my journey. The sun soon set, and I settled down to rest by a tree that was slightly off the path. But my rest was not as peaceful as I would have liked, because I dreamed about reviewing my journey again and again. I woke in the middle of the night and sat up to visualize a strong connection to home, as I knew that if I could focus fully on the desire to return there as quickly as possible, it would help me get there.

At dawn I stood up, and with Andy and Wyrme walked through what turned out to be the final group of trees to the path back home. When I arrived at my house and fell asleep, I resumed reviewing everything I had experienced on my journey, this time in a dream.

Throughout this dream I could hear the sound of the men clacking the river stones together. When I woke, I thought about this, including the reason I had set out on this journey in the first place, which was curiosity and a desire to have a greater range of experiences so I would be better prepared in case I would be returning to earth soon.

Even after my return home, the sound of the clacking stones I had heard during my journey kept coming back to me. While I had been fascinated by the men who looked like wizards doing their ritual, I realized it was the sound that had the most significance for me, because it was the same tone that I had heard when I had had the accident on earth that brought me to the other side, even though it had a more crystalline quality to it back then.

But by now I felt very different, as if I had completed necessary tasks to feel prepared for something else. However, I found it curious that one main result of my journey was a recollection of something that had brought me to this dimension.

As I thought about this, I felt something staring at me. I saw Andy watching me—not as a dog, but as a teacher who knew something. As our eyes met, it appeared that Andy nodded just a little to reveal that he understood something. In this moment, Andy did not try to hide the teacher I had suspected he was all along. This further impressed on me the fact that something had shifted. Hoping he might give me more information, I said, "If you have something to say, now is a good time to say it." But Andy's ears, which had been perked up, now dropped a little, as if someone had pulled a window shade down, and he reverted to his role of dog.

I looked at my skin to see if there was a blue glow indicating it was time to return to earth, but found nothing had changed. I left my house and looked at all the people I encountered. Everything looked the same. Apparently, nothing had changed except me, because of my journey.

Editor's note: When Galen was able to talk to his teacher about the mystery of the stone clackers, his teacher said the men clacking stones were the personas of the individuals who didn't believe there was an afterlife after death and that they had lived reflecting not necessarily atheism but the belief that death is the end of consciousness. The persona is a facet of the soul's experience that reflects light, color, and sound and directly assists in the earth dimension. But many times it is erroneously viewed as the *only* aspect of a person's identity. The persona is not the ambassador of our human life until we cross over. Galen stressed that the men were not trapped in their activities as a punishment but were working through a process, such as individuals who commit suicide do. But the fact that the men maintained a certain rhythm and connection with each other reflected the truth that there is a connection between everything.

The men didn't see Galen or Andy because they were so intently focused on contributing to the total rhythm.

The men's belief that consciousness does not survive death can, however, be disputed, because while energy can shift from one form to another, it is never destroyed. While scientists tell us matter is energy, the missing piece of that energy is *consciousness*. Some souls choose lives where they will not believe in anything beyond death, not because they are impaired, but because their soul and spirit need to go through a growth cycle. Galen said that this was likely why they looked like wizards—they had chosen an experience purposely to gain wisdom. And Galen perceived the men clacking stones as wizards because, for him, there was something symbolic about the wisdom of age and magic figures, as Galen was always interested in magic. I might have seen something else.

Galen also found out that the empty bubbles at the periphery of this activity were doorways for these individuals to exit when they had gained the necessary wisdom required, after which others would arrive to take their places. The strange images projected upon Andy were on Galen as well, but they really showed up on Andy, perhaps because Andy is more than the form he is portraying. Wyrme reflected the images even less than Galen, perhaps because it was a holographic being.

Further, Galen's teacher explained that the purpose of this realm was to allow those who no longer had any connection to the energy of their past lives to reconnect to these lives and the rhythm of the universe. The stones, which represent the bones of the earth, were the perfect instruments to play, as Galen's teacher explained, for individuals reuniting with the continuity of energy in the universe. Because light, color, and sound constitute the trinity of manifestation, and sound is the wave of energy that starts the movement of manifestation, in a sense these individuals were focusing on the basics, which may have been one reason they had such an impact on Galen.

For as long as I can remember, I have heard a high-frequency tone that I call "the cosmic crickets," which emits a rhythm out into the universe. Galen told me that this is what he saw as the men rubbed the stones together, and that my cosmic crickets and his river stones have the same sound. The sound is transmitted to me through the microcrystalline structures in my own bones. Since up to 50 percent of bone is made up of a modified form of the inorganic mineral hydroxylapatite, our bones can be passive receivers of energy and transmit signals without an external power source in much the same way early radios used crystals. I realized the sound was being received through my bones because I could modulate the sound by putting pressure on certain bones or changing their position.

EPILOGUE

I WAS DIVERTED FROM THE JOURNEY I had just been on when I met, in a class, earth ambassador Brock, an unusual being from a special class of incarnate beings that are holographic and materialize on the planet they are called to serve. He was preparing himself to take a different form without having transitioned, as I had done, via the death of a body. We became fast friends, because in many ways we were travelers with similar curiosities. During my final encounter with Brock, Andy departed at the same time Brock did, causing me to feel shock and anxiety, as I described in my first book.

Now looking back at my journey and the events that followed, I can see that Andy was truly being my teacher after I had felt changed following my journey, and in suddenly behaving like a teacher, he was also probably trying to communicate to me that it would soon be time for him to change as well. When both Brock and Andy left, I went through a lot in relation to my journey and my family dynamics, revisiting my connection to my mother and my father and better understanding aspects of my recent journey. I saw how patterns of behavior had kept everyone engaged in certain ways without awareness of negative consequences.

As a result of revisiting these past relationships and assessing the implications of Andy's sudden departure, I realized that Andy had created a beautiful cocoon around me that felt just like the protection my father and mother had provided to me on earth. While such protection had given me a sense of comfort and security, including Andy's pretense of being a dog, I could see that such protection had limited my awareness of everything. But when Andy left, and another protective layer was thus eliminated, I could better see the continuum from my earth life to the space I now occupy here in this dimension and became aware that the same messages are just given in different ways in the two dimensions. My teacher confirmed that my journey had changed me when I went to him to discuss my journey and get his assessment of my situation.

After I arrived and entered his house, I saw him standing in his study with his back turned to me, busy doing something. When he turned around, he had a surprised look on his face and said, "Galen, you have grown!" Having no idea what my teacher was talking about, I looked down at my hands and feet, which looked the same. But I could tell by my teacher's words and the look on his face that I had somehow matured. At first, I thought the change in me due to my journey had something to do with my subconsciously knowing that Andy would be leaving soon, and thus I had to be more independent. But I have now realized it is more than that—I now had the desire to be of service to others as part of my inner work.

While I am happy I have grown, at the same time I am sometimes frustrated, because I now often feel ready to return to earth, and I did not want to be left in my dimension alone without Andy's support to do my work of creating books to provide information for others. Every so often, I check my skin for blue coloring, hoping that it will soon be my time to go back to earth. I remember the conversation I had had in the forest with Glen, who explained that one has a sense of preparedness when one is about to return, and one receives a message indicating the time is coming. But as yet I have not received such a message. As I wait for my time to return to earth, I continue to focus on my deep desire to be of service to others, assisting those who are coming and going from this dimension and communicating information about other realms to my father—inspired by both Andy and Brock.

Editor's note: With the departure of Andy and Brock, Galen came to realize that he was alone. He still had Wyrme, but Wyrme is a creature no one truly understands, and Wyrme does not provide a sense of emotional safety or acceptance. At this point, Galen had to face many aspects of his new life more directly to gain the greater awareness needed to continue his growth. In addition, after he came back to his own realm following his journey, he found he could move about more freely to other realms where he could be of assistance to others without creating the confusion he sometimes had during his journey of difficulties trying to communicate with others who had entirely different beliefs. As Galen revisited his family dynamic, he felt deep grief about the fact that his parents had no reason to ever talk to each other. I had not seen his mother for four years, and at her request I was not communicating with her—although I had violated this request once, when Galen wanted her to know that his first book had been published, writing the following:

As Galen has built a bridge with me, he is also building one with you—he is communicating the changes that have come about in his transition from a physical human boy to who he is now. There is a difference between our two bridges, but there is still a very deep love and connection with you, and he is trying to make contact with you and bring this awareness up as well.

Just because I was the parent with whom he could be clearer doesn't mean that his love for his parents is unequal. He loves us both dearly. Galen could work his process out in front of me, but on earth he did not have that advantage with you, so that process became greater after he moved out of his body, because he could then see the deeper levels and connections.

His message to you and what he wants you to understand is that he could fight with me, he could disagree with me, but he was so afraid to hurt you that he didn't feel he could do that with you. His message now is that he loves you to his core and that he is okay and everything is alright. There isn't any blame or guilt or fear.

The book is as much for you as it is for me. It is a place to heal and get out a message to those whom he loves that says, "I am okay…not only am I okay, but I have a very full and clear life. You are not at fault, and I love you deeply. Deeply."

Galen told me that the three of us would reunite again at some point to align the energy among us if we wanted not to leave the family dynamic in a fractured state. He said if some of that work could be done now, the family dynamic would be a little more aligned.

As a result, I sent Galen's mother another email to let her know that if she ever needed anything, she should never hesitate to contact me, that she was still loved, and that she was not cut off from this part of her life.

Of all the souls available, it was her soul and Galen's that my soul chose, in a prebirth agreement, to work with on something deep and powerful, and that was the energy behind my attraction to her. While Galen's mother seems to be a frail butterfly here on earth, broken and fearful, I have been told that on the other side her soul and spirit are fearless and committed. As souls, we all make agreements to engage each other in order to create, learn, and gain awareness from that experience.

In service, I have also dedicated myself to be a bridge and keep an agreement going with my son by communicating with him while he is on the other side and helping to make the information he provides available to people on earth.

Galen has informed me that he is now assisting others as they cross over. He is not one of the teachers or guides who meet individuals at the threshold to the other side, for that is a position apparently reserved for angelic beings. But he was recruited at a great time of need to welcome those who came over in great numbers as a result of the 9.0 earthquake that hit Japan on March 11, 2011. He said while their arrival saddened him, he did his best to welcome them. Even though there is no language barrier on the other side, he said it probably helped that he could speak Japanese, having visited Japan on a school trip in eighth grade and studying the language for two years afterward. Galen continues to help heal brave souls who come together only to be separated again because of death and crossing over to his dimension.

ABOUT THE AUTHOR

Galen Stoller was in many respects an all-American kid. He liked going to theme parks and movies, visiting his grandparents, hamming it up at school, and hanging out with his friends. Steeped in the world of sci-fi/fantasy, he read the complete Harry Potter series, the Golden Compass/Dark Material series, and the Bartimaeus Trilogy. He also read the C. S. Lewis Narnia series over and over, except for the last book, in which all the protagonists were killed in a train accident—a volume he read once and never wanted to return to.

It was a train accident that would take Galen's earth life when he was sixteen years old. At the time, Galen was in eleventh grade at Desert Academy in Santa Fe, New Mexico, and starting to think about enrolling in college. An accomplished actor, he was about to perform the dual roles of Fagan and Bill Sikes in *Oliver*! He was an ethical vegetarian and helped train dogs for Assistance Dogs of the West. Because of this service, he was nominated posthumously for the 2008 Amy Biel Youth Spirit Award. Following the second anniversary of his passing, he asked his father to start writing *My Life after Life*, the first book in what he called the Death Walker series.

ABOUT THE EDITOR

K Paul Stoller, MD, started his medical career as a pediatrician and was a Diplomat of the American Board of Pediatrics for over two decades. Previously, in the early 1970s, he was a University of California President's Undergraduate Fellow in the Health Sciences, working in the UCLA Department of Anesthesiology and volunteering at the since disbanded Parapsychology Lab at the UCLA Neuropsychiatric Institute. He matriculated at Penn State and then completed his postgraduate training at UCLA.

His first published works, papers on psychopharmacology, came to print before he entered medical school. During medical school, he was hired to do research for the Humane Society of the United States and became involved in an effort to prohibit the use of shelter dogs for medical experiments, which made him very unpopular in certain circles when he published an article entitled "Sewer Science and Pound Seizure" in the *International Journal for the Study of Animal Problems.* He was then invited to become a founding board member of the Humane Farming Association, and served as science editor for the *Animal's Voice Magazine*, where he was nominated for a Maggie Award.

In the mid-1990s, after a friend, the head of Apple Computer's Advanced Technology Group, lapsed into a coma, Dr. Stoller began investigating hyperbaric medicine. Soon after, he started administering hyperbaric oxygen to brain-injured children and adults, including Iraqi vets and retired NFL players with traumatic brain injuries, also pioneering the use of this therapy for treating children with fetal alcohol syndrome. He was granted a lifetime Fellowship in the American College of Hyperbaric Medicine.

When his son was killed in a train accident in 2007, he discovered the effectiveness of the hormone oxytocin in treating pathological grief.

www.ingramcontent.com/pod-product-compliance
Lightning Source LLC
Chambersburg PA
CBHW042226160426
42811CB00117B/1022